*Peacock Publishing's Alchemy
Workbook Series*

I0168377

Alchemical Theory: Unlocking the Mysteries of Alchemy

By Frater M.T.O.

Frist Edition

First Printing, 2017

The publisher and author gratefully acknowledge Adam McLean for
permission to reprint the 109 alchemical processes, which was
researched and written by him.

Library of Congress Cataloging-in-Publication Data

ISBN: 978-1-944963-01-9 (pbk); 978-1-944963-02-6 (ebk)

Peacock Publishing
A Subsidiary of WillowHeart, LLC
www.peacockpublishing.net

DEDICATION

To my Omega, my beloved Soror MIMM, I love you, I adore you, I cherish you. You are the one for whom I waited for so many years of my life. You are my life, my love, my partner, my joy, my happiness, my everything. You truly are, the Rose upon the Altar of my Soul. Thank you for not only saving my life, but for making my life complete in so many ways. Without your love and encouragement, this book would not exist. To you, I dedicate this, my first book, with the words of the poem I wrote below.

The Rose Upon the Altar
You are the Rose upon the altar of my soul; I inhale the fragrance of your beauty--the beauty of your body, mind and spirit; I feel the warmth and heat of your passion and drive for our family, our magic and our oneness; I partake of the bread and salt of your world, our life together, living, loving and laughing in our present while planning for our future; I drink of the living waters of your soul, your teachings, your knowledge and your wisdom. And just as the bud of the Rose symbolizes the unopened potential of its true beauty, so does the golden rose symbolize the unopened potential of what lay ahead of us--living, loving and laughing together as a couple and as a family for the rest of this existence and beyond. I truly love you, completely and with all of my being. I love you, Soror MIMM.

Alchemical Theory

TABLE OF CONTENTS

INTRODUCTION: ABOUT THE ALCHEMY WORKBOOK SERIES AND THIS BOOK

About the Peacock Publishing Workbook series

The Peacock Publishing Workbook Series is designed as a collection of instructional texts meant to function not only as books, but as personal working journals, grimoires, and chronicles of one's own initiatory journey.

Whether the subject is Alchemy, Magic, Herbalism, Tarot, Freemasonry, or Egyptian Mysticism, each volume presents a clear, concise, and structured guide intended for serious students who desire practical understanding rather than abstract theory alone.

Each workbook provides foundational knowledge alongside step-by-step procedures for practical application. Whenever appropriate, detailed photographs and illustrations accompany the instructions to assist the practitioner in accurately performing the work. The goal is simplicity without dilution — clarity without oversimplification.

These texts are designed to remove unnecessary complication while preserving the integrity of the tradition. They are intended to serve as structured paths of study and practice, allowing the aspirant to move from theory to direct experience.

About this book

Numerous books on the "Royal Art" of Alchemy exist, yet many present the subject through highly symbolic, archaic, or deliberately obscured language. While historically significant, such works can make practical laboratory replication or structured spiritual application difficult for the modern student.

This volume was written to provide clarity.

The first section lays a firm conceptual foundation, explaining core alchemical principles in accessible language while interpreting the symbolic and procedural elements found in classical texts. This prepares the student for the second section: direct practical work.

The practical portion contains precise, step-by-step instructions, supported by photographs and clear explanations of each phase and process. Every effort has been made to recommend equipment and materials that are affordable and easily obtainable, often including common household alternatives when appropriate.

The spiritual exercises accompanying the laboratory work are likewise straightforward. No elaborate ritual tools or specialized attire are required — only sincerity, discipline, and a quiet place for reflection.

Alchemy is neither solely physical nor purely mental nor exclusively spiritual. It is the synthesis of all three. The laboratory work, contemplative exercises, and philosophical understanding presented here are designed to function together as a process of structured self-initiation.

Over years of teaching this material in classroom settings, the transformative effects of this integrated approach have been consistently observed. This book now presents that same structure in written form.

How to use this book

This volume serves as the foundational text within the Alchemy Workbook Series. It contains the essential principles and procedural understanding necessary for the practical work outlined in subsequent volumes.

While each workbook may be studied independently, students who intend to engage seriously in laboratory and spiritual practice are strongly encouraged to complete this volume first. It establishes the conceptual and practical framework upon which later work builds.

Approach the material methodically. Read carefully. Perform the exercises attentively. Record observations diligently.

Alchemy unfolds through experience.

SECTION 1: BASIC ALCHEMICAL THEORY AND KNOWLEDGE

CHAPTER 1:
INTRODUCTION TO
ALCHEMY

Introduction to Alchemy

What is alchemy? Alchemy, as understood by the modern world, was a pre-cursor of chemistry in the distant past. At one time, alchemy and chemistry were essentially the same science, however at some point, chemistry began to separate any concept of any sort of 'belief' from its basis and observations, and thus the more academic science of chemistry was born. Chemistry continued to evolve and became a science of its own, and for most supplanted the more archaic science of alchemy. Alchemy, however, has always been there, and from the substantial growth seen in the fields of Quantum Mechanics and Quantum Physics, we are now rediscovering the concept and the advantage of projecting ones 'belief' and observations, onto the actual experiment.

Alchemy has been the search for or the creation of the Philosophers Stone, a mystical and magical substance which could be used to then transform base metals into gold. Many believe that the alchemists sought to turn lead into gold by performing numerous experiments, processes and procedures upon the lead itself. While this may be true to some extent and at times, and certainly was the basis for some of their work, the true work of the alchemist was to create and perfect the Philosophers Stone. It was this stone that, when added to a solution containing the base metal, would act as a catalyst, initiating a reaction that would cause the actual transformation of the base metal, such as Lead, into Gold. This stone could not only transform base metals, but could also be used as an Elixir of Life, giving one the powers of rejuvenation and even immortality. By adding the stone to a solution, and then drinking it (after removing the stone of course), the alchemist would ingest a solution imbued with those same powers that changed lead into gold, thus changing his mortal or leaden life into an immortal or golden one. This process of transformation is just as effective upon the spiritual and mental planes as it is on the physical.

The work and process of the creation and discovery of this Stone was often termed the 'Magnum Opus', or Great Work. This Great Work was often seen by the uninitiated and misinformed as simply the quest to obtain gold or riches. However, to the initiated and practicing alchemist, the physical act of practical alchemy was only the external manifestation of the internal spiritual and esoteric alchemy. This internal or spiritual alchemy had the effect of changing not only the substance being transformed, but also the practitioner of this ancient science. As with so many things in the esoteric, mystical and magical worlds, alchemy was much more about the journey or the process of change and transformation, not solely concerned with the destination or its eventual outcome.

The transformation of the alchemist is accomplished via two distinct processes: the external or exoteric and the processes that are visual or could be observed; and the internal or esoteric processes, those that are invisible and can only be experienced. The external processes are the physical techniques and preparations used by the alchemist to produce herbal, mineral or metallic tinctures, elixirs, potions or stones, which each have a variety of uses. Internal processes are accomplished via meditations, visualizations, prayers, ritual, study, directing energies and other inner work undertaken by the alchemist in conjunction with the external processes. This dual approach creates a type of feedback loop, in which the internal methods reinforce the external methods, which in turn reinforce the future internal methods, and so on, creating a never-ending spiral of growth and energy.

External alchemy without internal alchemy is merely a form of specialized chemistry. Internal alchemy without external alchemy amounts to a type of personal or spiritual-mental development and form of self-help. In true alchemy, these two forms are symbiotic and inseparable and integrates the body, mind and spirit, just as the alchemist integrates the respective components of the salt, sulphur and mercury of the alchemical material. The sum of these two acting together, the external and the internal, is greater than the sum of its parts. While each alone may be a learning experience to create improvements and advancements in personal progression, utilizing them together has an exponential effect upon the alchemist.

Alchemical Stages, Processes and Principles
In alchemy, there are three primary working components that we will examine, typically termed stages, processes and principles. To some extent, these components may vary depending upon the specific path of alchemy (and with which teacher) you are studying.

When undertaking an alchemical experiment or work, at times you may use all the stages, all the processes and all the principles (at least, all the primary ones). However, there may also be times that you will not use all of them, but rather will use only a subset of them. In this process of alchemy, and for the purposes of this book, we will investigate Four Stages, Seven Processes and Three Principles.

In learning about the stages, processes and principles, the analogy of playing a board game will be used. This is not to imply that alchemy or alchemical work is any type of game or trifling thing. Yet by way of a high-level examination and explanation, the analogy works out rather well. There are several elements that are common to most board games. First is the player themselves, in this case the alchemist.

Then, there is the playing field or the game board. This is where the game is played out in its various steps, and in alchemy the stages are representative of the progress or state of the experiment. In alchemy, there are four primary stages. Think of the stages as differing parts of a playing field or a game board in this 'game' of alchemy. The game board is divided into 4 parts, and each of these 4 parts represents one of the 4 phases of alchemy. The phases could be representing the progress of the game, from beginning to end. The game begins with Nigredo (or the blackening); it moves on to Albedo (the whitening); next comes Citrinitas (the yellowing); and finally, the game moves to Rubedo (the reddening). As with many varieties of board games, sometimes the player moves his pieces forwards and sometimes backwards. Sometimes he may skip ahead a section or phase, while at others he may almost be near the end, and finds himself going all the way back to the beginning to start over. Working with the phases of alchemy is very much the same. While there is an order for the phases, we oftentimes will move backwards and forwards through these phases, as we move ourselves and our material basis, through a process of self-improvement and enlightenment.

Next, there are the game pieces, or the pawns, which are moved around the game board. These represent the actual players, or in the case of alchemy the 'parts' of the player (body, mind and spirit), as well as that of the material basis being worked with, be it herbal, mineral or metal. In alchemy, these three parts, the body, mind and spirit, are analogous to (and are termed) Salt, Sulphur and Mercury respectively. These three distinct pieces all start together at the very beginning. Once the material has been separated into the three pieces however, they may move independently of one another on and about the game board. Think about a game of checkers. When a piece reaches the far side of the board, the opponent 'crowns' your piece, where you now have two checkers. In using this analogy, think about having a checker with 3 crowns, one each for body, mind and spirit. They may move and act as a single piece, or split up into any variety of pieces (i.e. Salt/Sulphur as one and Mercury as another, or Sulphur/Mercury as one and Salt as another). In this way, we have a single piece, that can be split up into multiple pieces, so that the different representative pieces can be in different phases or have different processes enacted upon them separately, or they may also all have various processes enacted upon them while all together, as a single piece.

As an example, once the oils have been extracted from an herb or plant (the oils representing the mind or the alchemical Sulphur of the plant) using alcohol (the alcohol representing the spirit/life-giving force or alchemical mercury of the plant), we are left with the emptied husk of the physical herb (the physical remains representing the body or alchemical salt of the plant). The sulphur/mind and mercury/spirit of our herb may stay in the phase of Nigredo (the 1st phase), while we work on transforming and changing the salt/body of the herb through the processes of Calcination and Dissolution (passing into the phase of Albedo). Once the material that is being worked with is broken into the separate pieces, they can move independently, as well as be changed by the processes or plays that we will use for transformation. When recombined, they again function as a single unit, but are often separated and recombined multiple times throughout the various phases of alchemy. At the end of the 'game', typically these three components are reunited back into a single whole during the phase of Rubedo.

Lastly, we come to the plays or the moves that may be made on our game board, using the pieces or pawns. In the game of Chess, certain pieces may move in certain and specific directions or patterns.

Likewise, in alchemy, at different times and in different stages, the principles can be 'moved' in specific directions or patterns. These are the alchemical processes that we apply to the principles, that enact change upon them. In playing this 'game' of alchemy, the alchemist utilizes seven primary plays when moving the pawns around on the playing field and although there are numerous plays or processes (see Appendix A for a listing of 109 different alchemical processes), we will concern ourselves with seven primary ones for this workbook. The seven processes we will work with in this book are: Calcination; Dissolution; Separation; Conjunction; Fermentation; Distillation; and Coagulation.

So, in our 'game' of alchemy, we move our 3 pawns (the principle elements of body, mind and spirit of both the material and the alchemist) around on a game board divided into 4 parts (the 4 stages or Phases of alchemy). When we move them, we may move them in many different orders and multiple times around the same areas of the board, either separate or together. When we move our pieces, we do so by using specific moves or plays (the seven processes of alchemy). The pawns or pieces representing the principles, are moved by the action of the processes allowing them to move through the various phases of transformation.

In the external world of alchemy, we are dividing our material up into 3 parts or principles, the body, mind and spirit of the material, which is analogous to the body, mind and spirit of the alchemist. We physically transform these three parts through the 4 phases of alchemy, sometimes repeating a phase, or even skipping a phase depending on the material being transformed, or what the end goal or product will be. Moving our material from one phase to the next is done so by enacting the processes of alchemy upon the material, sometimes on each individual piece, sometimes on all the pieces at once, again depending on our material and the desired outcome.

In the internal world of alchemy, we have symbolically become the very physical parts that we are using in the external world. We have created a connection or bond between ourselves and our material. When we enact the processes of alchemy upon them, or when we transform them from one phase into another, that same process is mirrored within ourselves. As we continue the transformation of the pieces of our game, the transformation of ourselves moves along with it, in a type of sympathetic magic. We also have the added benefit that when the game is over, we are left with a substance that we may continue to use in order to repeat the process within ourselves daily if we so desire, for example by imbibing an alchemical tincture or elixir.

In truth, there are many ways to represent these various categories; in some traditions, there are 12 processes or even more, and many schools and traditions of alchemy now eliminate the Phase of Citrinitas completely. However, to lay the groundwork for this workbook series, and in keeping with our tradition of Alchemy, the traditional Four Stages, Seven processes and of course the Three Principals will be discussed.

So why do we play this 'game' called Alchemy? There are many reasons, but at a minimum alchemy is a philosophy that seeks to understand life, both animate and inanimate, the living and the lifeless, the seen and the unseen. Thus, the alchemist works with living things, such as herbs and plants, as well as the seemingly lifeless, such as minerals and metals, to understand the world around him. Alchemy IS a science and was the forerunner as well as the contributor to many other modern sciences, including chemistry, biology, psychology, medicine and even some forms of theology, as the alchemist works within a system or practice of belief, although not a dogmatic one. The personal beliefs of the alchemist are his own, and the phases, principles and processes become an overlay over his personal beliefs. As alchemy works with the body, mind and spirit, it looks at all aspects of the material, not only the physical aspects that we can see and feel. This is where alchemy and modern science differ, as modern science is concerned with the external, that which can be seen and touched, whereas alchemy, while also concerned with these same external aspects, also considers the interior qualities, senses and gifts.

CHAPTER 2: TYPES OF ALCHEMICAL WORK

There are several types of alchemical work, typically named after the type of material being transformed. As with the phases, processes and principles, some schools of alchemy may use more or less, combine some or even have others not listed here. We will investigate six primary types of alchemical work: Herbal Alchemy; Mineral Alchemy; Metallic Alchemy; Animal Alchemy; Magical Alchemy; and Spiritual Alchemy.

Herbal Alchemy

The term Herbal Alchemy is used to describe alchemical operations, which were traditionally performed on minerals or metals, being enacted upon herbal or plant material. The terms 'herbal alchemy' and 'spagyrics' are often used interchangeably in many works, although some would consider Spagyrics to be a sub-category of herbal alchemy. When looking at some of the ways in which you can work with plants and herbs in alchemy you can extract herbal tinctures; create the Primum Ens; create plant stones; and working with the spirit of the plants and herbs for spiritual growth. This last item has some crossover with what we call 'Magical Alchemy', and it has been categorized under that heading for this book.

Plants, just like minerals and metals, have their planetary correspondences, which helps to identify the physical and spiritual effectiveness of each individual herb. Plants, by their nature, are very easy and mostly forgiving to work with. If one is interested in pursuing a deeper understanding of alchemy, studying the alchemical work enacted upon plants can be an excellent place to start. Mineral, and particularly Metallic alchemy, often use caustic and dangerous chemicals. Indeed, a well-known alchemist, Israel Regardie, burned his lungs when fumes of Antimony escaped in his lab work and he breathed in the fumes. Afterwards, he gave his alchemy lab equipment to a friend, but for the rest of his life, he suffered from the effects of the accident, and used an oxygen tank often later in his life. This should be a warning not to avoid alchemy, but rather to practice with the utmost care and safety.

Within the realm of herbal alchemy, there are several sub-sets of alchemical work, including Tinctures/Spagyrics, The Primum Ens and Plant/Vegetable Stones.

Tinctures/Spagyrics

A tincture, sometimes also called a Spagyric is an herbal mixture, typically a medicine in the form of a tincture, elixir or tonic, produced by alchemical means and processes. These procedures often involve the processes of conjunction, dissolution, separation, calcination, and the extraction and transformation of specific components from the ash of the plant. All the constituents of the plant are utilized, not just the oils.

In short, Spagyrics is the use of the alchemical stages, processes and principles specifically enacted upon plant matter and material. Often this use of Spagyrics is for healing purposes, whether healing of body, mind or spirit, and it is the forerunner to many modern medicines. Thus, a Spagyric is a holistic form of natural medicine which treats the whole of the individual—body, mind and spirit.

Our modern pharmaceuticals are nothing but scientific creations based upon the elixirs, tinctures and potions of the alchemist, the medicine man, the witch doctor and the local village madman. In fact, in 2015 it was discovered that a 1,000-year-old recipe for an herbal treatment found in a book called "Bald's Leechbook", was more effective than modern antibiotics when fighting a specific type of staph infection[1]. The experiment was carried out using the scientific method, and was validated at multiple universities. The ancient alchemists and herbalists certainly understood the medicines with which they worked, and were well aware of their capabilities.

Modern aspirin (or acetylsalicylic acid) dates to ancient Egypt. Hippocrates referred to the use of a salicylic tea to reduce fevers around 400BCE. Modern medicine now artificially manufactures this natural pain reliever, but where did our ancient predecessors find it? In the bark of the White Willow tree. Thus, the modern-day alchemist may create a tincture of Willow Bark, which when completed as an alchemical tincture, not only has the physical benefits of pain relief, but is so much more potent due to its accompanying effects upon the mind and spirit as well. It is also the belief of most alchemists that a natural cure is of course more beneficial and more easily absorbed and used by the body than a synthetic substance.

Today's modern pharmaceuticals are targeted to very specific symptoms and causes. These medicines are much more specific and of a stronger nature than our natural immune systems and how our bodies are accustomed to being treated naturally. Hence, while their nature of being so specific is somewhat like a surgical scalpel in its base nature, it's strength and efficacy is more like using a jackhammer on our bodies and immune systems. Often, our body only needs a nudge in the right direction to allow it's natural healing mechanisms to kick in. Herbal medicines are more holistic in nature, and give the

---

[1] http://www.bbc.com/news/uk-england-nottinghamshire-32117815

body that needed 'nudge' in the right direction. This is easier on the body, more natural and for those interested in a holistic sense of health, makes much more sense.

For example, if one has high cholesterol, there are a multitude of pharmaceuticals that can be taken. These are very specifically targeted to reduce cholesterol found within the blood system. However, they also introduce numerous side effects, such as muscle pain and soreness, inflammation, liver and kidney damage and more. These medications are so powerful, they are like hitting the body with a sledgehammer to have the simple effect of lowering cholesterol. Using an herbal tonic, made up for example of Garlic, Turmeric, Skullcap and Ginger (all herbs believed to help in lowering cholesterol within the blood system), is a more natural and moderate way to reduce cholesterol. There are few side effects and it can be just as powerful in lowering cholesterol as pharmaceutical medicines. This has a gentler effect upon the body, that does not assault the bodily systems like a sledgehammer, but rather is more like using scalpel and forceps, certainly a much gentler way. That being said, before discontinuing the use of any prescription medications in favor of an herbal treatment, you should always consult with your physician as well as an herbalist in coming up with a plan to monitor your progress during the transition period. Never stop medications given to you by a medical professional until you have a chance to discuss the details with them.

Often, alchemy consisted of utilizing metallic substances, such as lead or mercury. Many of the chemicals used for various processes of transmutation of such metals, can be caustic and dangerous. In our modern world, Spagyrics is one method of working within the confines of the alchemical process, enabling the alchemist to be able to perform practical alchemy, both external and internal, exoteric and esoteric, in a much safer environment and on substances that are not dangerous to living things. Many alchemists begin working with Spagyrics and graduate to mineral/metallic alchemy after gaining a certain level of experience.

With Spagyrics, care must still be taken, as some herbs and plant materials can be harmful, some even deadly, but the processes themselves are relatively safe. One example of a resultant Spagyric formulation is typically called a tincture, and it has a transformative effect upon the alchemist, not only through the process of its creation, but also through its use as an herbal remedy, to heal mind, body and spirit.

The Primum Ens

The Primum Ens is seen as one of the most powerful rejuvenating medicines of the Plant Kingdom, and therefore is classified under Herbal Alchemy. The 'Primum Ens' is considered to be a thing in its first beginning, its first entity or Prima Materia; an invisible and intangible spiritual substance, which may be incorporated in some material vehicle. The Primum Ens is a type of tincture made with tartar oil as the first solvent, and then later with the spirit of wine. An herbal tincture, or Spagyric, begins with all 3 Principles, the Salt, Sulphur and Mercury, whereas the Ens does not, only the Sulphur and Mercury are present (sometimes referred to as a 'vulgar tincture'). Like tinctures and other scientific arena, there are multiple ways and different processes for creating the Primum Ens. In some of these, the outcome can certainly be somewhat different, but that makes them no less valid.

Plant/Vegetable Stones

In the world of alchemy, the Alchemical Stone is the most sought-after accomplishment. There are different types of stones, as well as different uses and attributions to each stone. There are artificial stones, in which a neutral 'Salt' substance is infused with the herbal oils and attributes of a plant. These often will have a use such as mental, magical or something more from the unseen world. These are a great way to familiarize oneself with the process of creating a stone, and they have benefits and uses in their own right. Next, there are plant stones, which also contain specific energies, such as creating an elemental or a planetary stone. Additionally, plant stones are often used in healing, both energetic for the mind and spirit, as well as physical healing and regenerative effects upon the body. The plant stones could be thought of as an extremely concentrated and potent tincture, in a solid form. Creating the artificial and plant stones have amazing effects upon the body, mind and spirit of the alchemist, and represent a certain level of adepthood within herbal alchemy. While an alchemist is never 'finished' with his alchemy (until and unless he completes the Magnum Opus and walks off into immortality), completing the creation of a certain number of plant stones represents a graduation of sorts, and certainly signifies a high level of accomplishment.

Working with plants within Alchemy can be a lifelong pursuit. It also offers the opportunity to work within the Alchemical processes in a safer environment and using materials that are less volatile than when typically working with minerals or metals. Once mastered, the process can be repeated and continued, as the number of herbs available for use are practically infinite.

Mineral Alchemy

In mineral alchemy, the phases and processes of alchemy are enacted upon various minerals and stones. Like all other forms of alchemy, you can extract oils, infuse elixirs and create stones from the various minerals and stones found in our world. There are a lot of similarities between mineral and metallic alchemy, but there are also some differences as well. In both, stronger chemicals are typically used than that found in herbal alchemy, to perform the extractions.

There are thousands[2] of different minerals found through this world and universe, each one unique in its expression of the four elements and three principles of the ancient alchemists. Minerals, just

---

[2] About 6100 Minerals currently, with 30-50 new ones added each year.

like plants and metals have their planetary correspondences, which helps to identify the physical and spiritual effectiveness of each individual mineral oil or spirit. Extracting and then working with different mineral oils and creating mineral elixirs and stones is a new way for many to commune and work with crystals, gems, or stones that you may have found intriguing or feel a pull to work with.

When working with minerals, some examples of the type of work that you can do is to create stone elixirs, extract the oil of various stones and crystals, as well as create mineral stones. Artificial stones are created from a neutral substance (such as sea salt), and then are infused with the oils of other plants or stones. These are a great way to begin to learn to work with the 'stones' in alchemy, and is often a first step in that me process.

Metallic Alchemy

In metallic alchemy, the phases and processes of alchemy are enacted upon various metals. The ancient alchemists assigned a specific metal to each of the seven ancient planets. These metals formed a large base of the material that was used in metallic alchemy, but there were certainly more than seven that were used. Like all other forms of alchemy, you can extract oils, infuse elixirs and create stones from the various metals. Of course, the most famous alchemical experiment of all is that to turn base metals, such as Lead, into precious metals, such as Silver and Gold.

To extract the oils of metals, specific laboratory processes known to ancient alchemists must be employed. There are a few different methods by which this can be accomplished. Each process is slightly unique to the metallic material that is used. The first method is known as the Acetate Path. This path takes purified metals and converts them into acetate crystals. These crystals are then crushed and distilled to render the soul and spirit of the metal at hand. The second method is one of oil extraction or pulling. Using this method, the soul of a particular metal is attracted into a type of spirit. The spirit can then be distilled off to leave the pure essence of the metal behind.

Overall, these processes can take months to complete as to bring these essences to perfection. The material used, time taken, safety precautions used and the strict attention to detail are all extremely important when practicing metallic alchemy. Metallic alchemy is often considered the most powerful and most potent form of alchemy, but it can also be the most dangerous. Not only are dangerous chemicals used, and toxic fumes often released during the alchemical processes, but ingesting or testing the materials themselves can cause potential concerns.

Animal Alchemy

Animal Alchemy is the use and application of alchemical principles and processes enacted upon living (or formerly living) material. It is a school of alchemy that was popular in ages past, but due to suppression based upon its moral taboo, is not often found in most modern schools of alchemy. If we examine the frontiers of medicine, often medicines were derived from plants and minerals, and then often tested on animals before proceeding to human trials. In today's modern world, we find the use of animal tissue, such as the cells of a dried pigs bladder, used to stimulate human stem cells in order to stimulate the re-growth of a finger[3] or limb. There have also been cases of using fetal stem cells, or even having your own stem cells used, to grow new organs[4]. There is healing to be found in nearly everything in existence, from plants, minerals and metals to parts and systems of animal and human tissue.

The school of Animal Alchemy is often ignored. Sometimes it is because of moral or societal taboos due to the possible image of

---

[3] http://news.bbc.co.uk/2/hi/7354458.stm

[4] http://discovermagazine.com/2014/jan-feb/05-stem-cell-future

animal or even human mistreatment. In other cases, it may be a religious taboo, in the case of using human or animal tissue or blood in some type of magical act or ritual of transformation. Regardless of the reason, there are moral and ethical ways of working in the school of Animal Alchemy and we can even learn both through observation as well as transformation in working with the animal kingdom. We can observe the transmutation of blood, tissue, hair, urine and other bodily fluids, and learn about the transmutation of ourselves into something greater. We do not have to necessarily do harm to ourselves or other creatures. For example, a lock of hair from your own head or that of an animal, can be obtained without any trauma or damage to either. Likewise, using your own urine in a transmutation, while perhaps not appealing, can be done without harm to anyone or anything. These types of experiments can lead us to new insights and learn about the phenomenal way in which our physical bodies can work and heal.

Though in no way complete, here are some of the parts and pieces that can be used in animal alchemy:

- Hair
- Milk
- Eggs
- Honey
- Beeswax
- Urine
- Blood
- Skin
- Teeth/Bones
- Reproductive/Sexual Fluids
- Excrement

It should go without saying (but must be said) that most, if not all of these materials, will be for the benefit of observation. Rarely if ever would you ever ingest something without CAREFULLY and KNOWINGLY understanding the potential consequences, and understanding exactly what ingredients were used and what they may have transformed into. This is a very important tip to understand, and you should always consider the safety ramifications of ingesting anything, but particularly any material produced via animal alchemy.

Although it too crosses over into Magical Alchemy, the last area of animal alchemy to discuss is the creation of the Homunculi. Homunculi is Latin for "little man" (from the masculine diminutive form of homo, "man") and is a representation of a small human being. Popularized in sixteenth century alchemy and brought to the public eye via nineteenth century fiction, it has historically referred to the creation of a miniature, yet fully formed human. The concept has roots in earlier Folklore, as well as Alchemical and Rosicrucian traditions as well. The homunculi has also been compared to the golem of Jewish mysticism. Though the specifics outlining the creation of the golem and homunculus are very different, the concepts are somewhat similar. One could almost say that the Homunculi was the ancient and alchemical attempt at a form of genetic manipulation. However, the Homunculi is said to be devoid of a soul, and is only an animated body.

There are some written and traditional teachings on the purpose of creating a Homunculi, and there are even more to be found if you read between the lines and understand the alchemical principles. Homunculi are said to bestow various gifts and powers upon their creators, depending on the materials and form of their creation. As with nearly anything in magic and alchemy, there is a real, practical and viable method and need for the physical creation and manifestation of these magical entities, beings or creatures. There are specific lessons to be learned from the very act and process of creation of these types of entities. There is almost certainly also a metaphorical reason for the creation of these entities as well, and that physical process of creation teaches the metaphorical lesson that is meant for the soul. Some items to consider the creation of these beings as a metaphor are: sex magic; the creation and regeneration of oneself and the soul; and using these processes to come into touch with one's Holy Guardian Angel, as well as deity itself, thus mimicking the creative and life-giving process that was enacted upon ourselves.

Animal alchemy, while often given a poor reputation due to many of its practices being seen as taboo, is a very advanced form of alchemy. Some may have a moral and/or spiritual conflict or issue when working within this system. If so, then there is a very important piece of advice for them. Don't work that system. If a conflict is seen, then simply avoid working with animal alchemy and continue to work with some of the other schools and types of alchemy. There are enough lessons and alchemical work within any of the alchemical schools, to keep the average person busy for a lifetime, if not several. Choosing the area in which you would like to pursue and specialize is part of your personal alchemical journey, and can only be determined by the practitioner, with perhaps the aid and advice of a teacher, spirit guide, holy guardian angel or deity.

Magical Alchemy

There are numerous definitions of the word 'magic', and it could easily consume (and has) entire books on just how the word 'magic' can be defined. We will keep it simple and say that magic is some type of supernatural or even almost miraculous event, typically done at the will of the magician. Thus, magical alchemy would be some type of supernatural event or action that is performed by means of the phases, processes and principles of Alchemy. When using the phrase 'spiritual alchemy', we are typically saying that the alchemical processes are being enacted upon ourselves for spiritual growth. Typically, when we talk about 'magical alchemy', we are using the phases, processes and principles of alchemy on something external to ourselves. This does not mean that spiritual growth cannot occur from the outcome of these processes, quite the opposite in fact.

However, instead of our spiritual nature being the object of the experiments, some other object or entity is the object of those experiments.

A few examples of Magical Alchemy are:

- Using the Planetary Stones to get in touch with the Astrological energies of the Planets
- Summoning and working with the great Spirit of various Herbs and Plants
- Creating an Alchemical Servitor or Spirit
- Creating and working with a Homunculus (or an artificial human being)

Often, the terms 'Magic' and 'Alchemy' are used together or interchangeably. In reality, they are very different practices, with a common ground between them. Thus, there is magic in alchemy, and there is alchemy in magic, but they each can stand alone as their own art or science.

Spiritual Alchemy

The practice of alchemy is one of transformation. In fact, for many, those words are interchangeable. If we accept that alchemy is transformation, then the act of cooking and making a complete dish from various ingredients is alchemy; attending a positive thinking workshop, where you change certain directions in your life is alchemy; and lastly, hopefully, the act of creating an alchemical tincture or oil is also alchemy. There are many modern mystery schools that teach what they call 'spiritual alchemy'. Certainly, they can do that, whether it amounts to a type of positive thinking, or whether they merely apply the alchemical principles and their nature to the path of life, both could be considered a form of 'spiritual alchemy'.

It is the opinion of this author, and thus the stance taken in these books and workbooks, that those two paths, physical or practical alchemy and spiritual alchemy, are intertwined and symbiotic. The practice of physical or external Alchemy without the spiritual is merely a form of specialized chemistry. Spiritual alchemy without the external or physical alchemy amounts to a type of personal or spiritual/mental development and form of self-help. In true Alchemy, these two forms are symbiotic and inseparable and integrates the Body, Mind and Spirit, just as the Alchemist integrates the respective alchemical components of the Salt, Sulphur and Mercury of the material. The sum of these two acting together, the external and the internal, is greater than the sum of its parts. While each alone may be a learning experience, and create improvements and advancements in personal progression, utilizing them together has an exponential effect upon the alchemist.

Consider the process of creating an herbal tincture, which is the subject of one of the available workbooks. As the alchemist goes through the physical process of creating a tincture, he gives energy, purpose, and life to his mixture. At the end of the process, the tincture itself has become a type of talisman, with an energetic life of its own. At this point, the alchemist now imbibes the tincture. The taking of the tincture internally, combined with the internal spiritual work performed during the creation of the tincture, provides the alchemist with healing benefits of body, mind and spirit, thus elevating him to a new level. This healing process radiates outward from the inside of the alchemist, as well as causing changes in the aura or energetic field of the alchemist. When the alchemist creates another tincture, during this new process the previous changes that have caused change in the aura of the alchemist will now have an influence the creation of the new tincture. It is affected by the internal changes of the alchemist, including the changes in the aura, while subsequent healing experiences increases the potency and effects of the next tincture, and so on.

Is it possible to have the experience and transformation of Alchemy without practicing the physical practices? Sure. Is it possible to become a professional football player merely by studying playbooks and analyzing films? While it may be possible, it would be extremely difficult. The image of the winged and legged Ouroboros demonstrates the strength of true Alchemy.

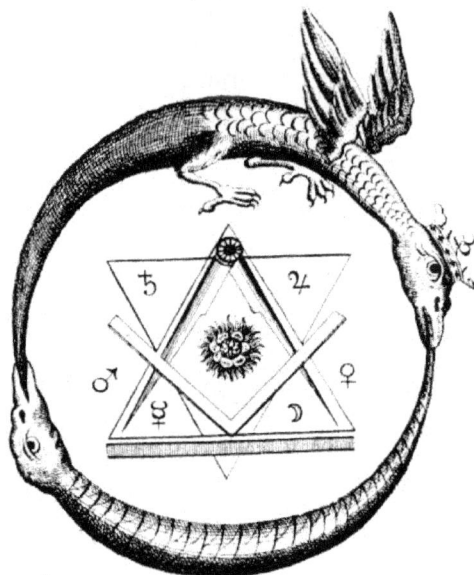

The lower or ground serpent represents the physical acts and practice of Alchemy, which feeds the spiritual process of personal transformation, as represented by the winged serpent across the top. These two are symbiotic in nature and feed off of one another. Each physical act, mirroring itself within the soul and spirit of the practitioner, while that change within the practitioner then influences the next physical act and so on.

So, while some schools advertise the teaching of Spiritual Alchemy, that is not a specific workbook that you will find offered here. All of our workbooks are blended and cohesive patterns which utilize physical and spiritual alchemy to cause both physical and spiritual transformation. Spiritual alchemy is certainly a principle used in our teachings and workbooks, but not as a stand-alone course and not separate from physical alchemy.

CHAPTER 3:
THE FOUR PHASES OF
ALCHEMY

Within alchemy, there are four phases. These phases are levels of evolution, maturity, or progress through which the material, as well as the alchemist, travel during the process of transformation. If you will remember, with the process of alchemy being likened to a board game, the phases represent the actual game board, the place where the actions themselves will take place. Each of these four phases of alchemy will be explored in depth.

Nigredo

Nigredo, or 'the blackening', in the alchemical sense refers to the putrefaction, decay and decomposition of the ingredients. This decay may take one of several forms. It most often occurs when the inner fire of the matter is activated and it begins to decompose or putrefy. The substance is broken down and reduced to its original components from which it was made. This is often seen today in the process of composting. In working with a compost heap or barrel, a heat can be felt emanating from the composted material. This is the internal fire of the organic matter activating via a chemical reaction, causing a more rapid decomposition of the matter. In some cases, whether due to the nature of the material or based on the strictures of time, sometimes an external fire may also be applied to assist in the ignition of the internal fire. This can be seen, as an example, in the lighting of a campfire. The wood itself if left alone will decompose over time into a different substance. But to ignite the internal fire of the wood and to allow it to completely burn, requires and external flame to be applied. Once the external flame is applied, the wood continues to burn and fundamentally changes its makeup and chemical structure until what is left in the form of the ashes, no longer resembles the original log or material. This external flame accelerated the natural decomposition by igniting the internal fire of the substance. Nigredo is sometimes called "blacker than the blackest black" and the process is often called 'cooking', due to the heat that is generated.

When looking at mythology with an eye to the phase of Nigredo, it exemplifies the difficulties that the hero must often overcome along the path of his journey. For example, Hercules had to accomplish twelve nearly impossible tasks. Orpheus had to enter the gates of Hades, calm Cerberus and find Hades and Persephone. Perseus, for example, had to find and overcome Medusa to gain a weapon with which to defeat the Gorgon. In many of these stories in mythology, as well as in real life, the hero traditionally encounters monsters, demons or often even shades of the dark side of himself. In ancient initiations, the candidate was said to undergo difficult, painful and even dangerous scenarios as a form of testing. This trial is sometimes called or equated to 'The Dark Night of the Soul', and represents the lowest of the low. The individual has reached a point from which the only way to go is up. This is a fundamental basis of Nigredo.

In alchemy, one of the symbols of Nigredo is a decapitated head and often also a raven or a raven's head. It is very appropriate that one of the tasks of Perseus was to decapitate Medusa, to use her head in slaying the Gorgon. The act of learning how to find and defeat her was part of his quest, and represented one of the trials of Nigredo. The symbol of the severed head represents the death of every man, but also the death of his ignorance, fears and doubts. Only when we release the bonds of ignorance, intolerance and weakness can a man claim his rightful inheritance. Our ignorance, fears and doubts blinds us to the truth, even though it may be directly in front of us. However, once these negative traits are purged from the soul, only then may the glimmer of enlightenment be seen that lay ahead. Hercules, in his fifth task, was made to clean King Augeas' stables by diverting the course of a river through them. This cleansing is symbolic of the cleansing of all of the impurities within oneself during this phase of Nigredo, before continuing with the Hero's journey, and the alchemical process of transformation.

The metal most often associated with Nigredo is Lead. Since turning 'Lead' or other base metals into Gold was the metaphorical quest of alchemy, Lead is often seen as the starting point, the basis or material upon which the alchemist will begin to enact his alchemical processes. Also, the color of Lead is a dark grey to black color, and thus is a fitting representative of the state of Nigredo.

When experiencing this cleansing or 'Dark Night of the Soul', the individual is put through a difficult and trying journey. These trials may take the form of physical, mental, emotional, spiritual or even a combination of many or all of them. These trials are put in place to cause the individual to develop a sense of self-awareness and self-realization. Seeing oneself from another perspective for the first time, as well as the truth of the world around them, rather than through the mirror of the ego and social constructs built up around them, is often startling. When the individual sees themselves for what they truly are, the changes that must be made are often obvious. The issue then becomes instituting change within oneself and overcoming the obstacles that this process of change requires. This deep and inward reflection is a trigger mechanism. It acts as the external flame, which ignites the internal alchemical fire, thus beginning the putrefaction and breakdown of the negative traits, cleansing and making room for the positive changes that are on the horizon.

The process of change is all too often accompanied by pain. Human beings tend not to like pain and so as a whole, generally do not often enjoy change. The process of alchemical change is very often a painful process. There is typically no recourse, those who have dedicated themselves to the path and true change endure and pass through their Dark Night of the Soul, while those who have taken on the task as merely a fad or as a popular thing to do, will generally fall by the wayside. For those who leave the path early, often these trials will stop, and they will not experience any further challenges or changes, although occasionally the trials and tests will continue at least for a time. Those who persevere and endure to the end will reap rewards, see changes and experience things that are often far beyond their expectations.

Let's say, for example, that someone is struck upon the head and dumped into a deep well. Lying at the bottom, disoriented and alone, the person may literally not even know which way is up. Slowly, gaining their bearings they stand up in the obscure darkness and mud, feeling around themselves in an attempt to guess at their current situation. This is Nigredo, and is truly when you have hit 'rock bottom'. As they begin to feel around them, and their eyes adjust and they become acclimated to their situation, they may even hazard to guess where they are. They may attempt to climb out, but will likely find that extremely difficult and dangerous in the dark. Until the light comes, that light that is found in the next phase of Albedo, they may choose to wait it out, to ponder their circumstances, to consider their options and perhaps to begin mentally conceiving of a way out of the dark space in which they find themselves. However, in this dark night of the soul, the person may not even know which way is the way out. They must have the patience and perseverance to allow the darkness to pass, and to move into the Light of Albedo.

This phase is typically the most painful one, and many who join occult orders, organizations or perhaps who choose to undertake magical or mystical work on their own, often find issues relating to Nigredo occurring not long after beginning the work, and sometimes even just preceding it. The action of making a choice to follow a new spiritual path will have its own effects upon the astral plane, which will often begin the process of change, even in advance of initiation or practical work. The mere process of considering and just beginning to do magical or mystical work will cause the impurities within themselves to begin to manifest, and the change that it takes to overcome them, can be painful. Many give up and choose not to continue, even though the journey has yet to truly begin. Those who do continue, find that the experience, while painful, is life changing, and is a defining experience for them personally.

Per some sources the phase of Nigredo is said to last forty days. The number 40 has a spiritual significance in many paths and traditions. Here are some examples of the number 40 found among various spiritual traditions:

- During the flood of Noah, the rains fell for 40 days and nights (Genesis 7:4).
- The Hebrew people lived in the Sinai desert and ate manna for 40 years. (Exodus 16:35).
- Moses was with God on Mount Sinai for 40 days and nights (Exodus 24:18).
- Moses was again with God for 40 days and 40 nights (Exodus 34:28).
- The spies searched the land of Canaan for 40 days. (Numbers 13:25).
- Therefore, God made Israel wander for 40 years (Numbers 14:33-34).
- 40 stripes was the maximum whipping penalty (Deuteronomy 25:3).
- Israel did evil; God gave them to an enemy for 40 years (Judges 13:1).

- Goliath challenged the Israelites for 40 days before David faced him. (1 Samuel 17:16).
- David then reigned over Israel for 40 years (2 Samuel 5:4, 1 Kings 2:11).
- The holy place of the temple was 40 cubits long (1 Kings 6:17).
- 40 baths (a measurement) was the size of the lavers in Temple (1 Kings 7:38).
- The sockets of silver are in groups of 40 (Exodus 26:19 & 21).
- Solomon reigned same length as his father; 40 years (1 Kings 11:42).
- Elijah had one meal that gave him strength 40 days (1 Kings 19:8).
- Ezekiel bore the iniquity of the house of Judah for 40 days (Ezekiel 4:6).
- Egypt to be laid desolate for 40 years (Ezekiel 29:11-12).
- Ezekiel's (symbolic) temple is 40 cubits long (Ezekiel 41:2).
- The courts in Ezekiel's temple were 40 cubits long (Ezra 46:22).
- God gave Nineveh 40 days to repent (Jonah 3:4).
- Jesus fasted 40 days and nights (Matthew 4:2).
- Jesus was tempted 40 days (Luke 4:2, Mark 1:13).
- Jesus remained on the earth for 40 days from the resurrection until the ascension (Acts 1:3).
- In Hinduism, many prayers consist of 40 verses and fasting for 40 days is common.
- In Islam, Elijah spent 40 days in the wilderness
- In Islam, Muhammad was 40 years old when he received a revelation from Gabriel and the mourning period of 40 days.
- In Christianity, Lent consists of the 40 days preceding Easter.
- Many students will allow the first phase or maceration of a tincture, which is a Spagyric form of Nigredo, to last for 40 days.

These, and many other examples as well (there are numerous Old Testament examples of kings or rulers ruling for 40 years that were not included in the above list) show that the number 40 holds some special spiritual significance. When considering the phase of Nigredo, while the number '40' or other numbers of spiritual or magical significance may apply, it is important to remember that the duration for personal change and the Dark Night of the Soul have no set timeframe. The trials and challenges will work themselves out in a time suitable to the individual, and often there is little control over when this period may end. It may be longer or shorter, depending upon the preparation and willingness of the individual to embrace and accept the change.

Due to its nature, Nigredo is typically the most difficult of all of the phases. The Dark Night of the Soul is a trial that once undergone, will never be forgotten. However, the lessons learned and experiences gained when traversing that chasm is one that would never be traded for anything. The wisdom and experience acquired by such an event is beyond anything that can be taught, read in a book or learned in any other fashion.

It is also important to understand that choosing to follow a path such as alchemy that focuses on personal change, growth and spiritual development, it is much like climbing a mountain with a series of plateaus. In the journey towards spiritual growth and enlightenment, in alchemy one will travel through the phases of Nigredo, Albedo and Rubedo, only to find that while growth and improvement have occurred and a new level of enlightenment achieved, we have only reached a plateau of our progress, and before us is another part of the mountain. We then repeat the process again and again, until we finally reach the pinnacle of the mountain, which often takes a lifetime, or possibly even multiple lifetimes, to obtain.

One of the best admonitions when going through this phase is simply, to be aware of its presence. Knowing that trials are coming or that obstacles will be appearing doesn't help to avoid them, however it can help to understand the process and to aid in one's perseverance to the path. However, having a pious or humble attitude towards this knowledge is also highly advised. Going in with the attitude of meeting the trials head on, and that you will conquer them with strength is surely an exercise in futility. In a vast majority of cases, the trials will present themselves in a format or form that will be completely unexpected, formerly unexperienced and often will come out of nowhere, always taking the person by surprise.

Nigredo, while often challenging and almost always painful, is one of the most rewarding phases. Overcoming obstacles and trials lends a wisdom and insight not gained in any other way. Beginning to ascend out of the darkness is truly fulfilling and more worthwhile than one may have expected.

Figure 2.1-Alchemical Plate showing the phase of Nigredo

This old alchemical drawing demonstrates the process of Nigredo. The alchemist's body, having been buried, is undergoing the process of decomposition and putrefaction. The black crow or raven, often seen as a symbol for the phase of Nigredo, is perched upon the alchemist's body. As a carrion eater, the matter that he devours is often putrefied, and thus he stands watch over the man, or the matter to be decomposed. The two winged figures coming out of the body are the soul (Sulphur) and the spirit (mercury), which when combined with the body present (salt) give us the three principles of alchemy, and constitute what we would call 'Life'.

The planets, viewed within the Hexagrams, are all related to the various stages and processes of the alchemical work, but also represent the energies present by which the entombed body will be transmuted. The Saturn hexagram is colored black as the planet Saturn rules over Nigredo. Both the color black and the metallic lead are often associated to the planet Saturn.

The Sun and Moon are seen as the opposing forces that are to be united via the alchemical work, the masculine and feminine aspects, and at this phase they are in opposition to one another, each working separately and imposing their influence in a singular fashion, without the aid or knowledge of the other. They also represent the latter stages of Albedo and Rubedo. The fire and air are the elements stimulating the decomposition, the air blowing on the hot embers of the fire, heating the crucible in which the alchemist lays.

The circle or crucible, emphasizes the idea of union or unification, with no beginning and no end, indicating the repetitive nature of Solve et Coagula. It also represents the vessel in which the decomposition of Nigredo takes place.

Albedo

Albedo, or the Whitening, is the second phase of alchemy. In the stage of Albedo, the alchemical fires of Nigredo have transformed the material and have begun to change its fundamental form and essence into a higher state or vibration. The external flame has been applied, and has ignited the internal fire of the material, causing it to rise out of the darkness and obscurity of Nigredo. The result of this change is represented by the whiteness of Albedo. The hero has passed through the test and challenges that were placed in his path, and he is now continuing towards the final goal of his quest.

Some have considered this change into whiteness to be the final goal. Albedo, however, is still just the start. To return to the analogy of being thrown into a well at midnight, Albedo is when the sun finally arises, and the person at the bottom of the well can finally catch a glimpse of light at the top of the well. He can see his surroundings and now determine his condition and location, but he is still currently at the bottom of the well. Once the sun begins to rise, and the light begins to shine above, then the person at the bottom of the well can now at least see a path out of the well. Looking up at the white light shining above gives one the hope of transformation and ascension through the phase of Albedo.

There is light at the end of the tunnel (or at the top of the well), and a plan is now beginning to take shape for climbing out of the depths of the well. Places for handholds, footholds and a safe route to traverse can now be identified, planned and thought out. The path is now becoming clear and the changes that need to be made to enable one to begin to climb and ascend towards the light have been made, or are at least in progress. At this point, a certain level of self-enlightenment has been achieved. The path ahead is set, the steps to climb out of Nigredo towards the Light have been determined and made apparent and the plan is now ready to be enacted.

This is the internal fire, the self-knowledge and enlightenment of what must be done to get out of the dark pits of Nigredo. Being able to imagine climbing out of the well and into the Light is itself, a form of enlightenment. It is the first step onto the path out of the darkness and into the light. This level of enlightenment is not the final one, of course; but rather an understanding of what tasks lie ahead, what must be done to move forward and often receive just a glimpse of that final state, of being out of the well at long last, which only motivates and inspires the individual even more.

Caution is advised at this point. Sometimes we may think that we are more advanced, further along or privileged in some way, when we are not. This is often seen in the person undergoing the changes in a form of self-deception; thinking that one is further along, more advanced or has experienced massive growth, when the reality is that the breakdown has occurred, and that the real growth is just beginning, but the completion of that growth and into the final stage is yet some ways off. Determining a plan of action to climb out of the well is a great accomplishment, but the person must not pat themselves on the back just yet. Having a plan and enacting the plan are very different things. The plan must still be executed, and while it may be a good or even a great plan, the person may still encounter wet or slippery rocks and handholds, or rocks that when used, crumble or dislodge from the well. This can delay the ascent from out of the well, or cause them to fall backwards. It is the gold or red state of Rubedo, that is the end objective, not the white state of Albedo. Albedo is merely the beginning of the change, and the true unification is yet to occur.

Following the harrowing, chaotic nature and experiences of Nigredo, it is necessary for the purification provided by Albedo which is sometimes literally referred to as "Ablutio" or the washing away of impurities by the "Aqua Vitae", the vital waters, better known as the "Waters of Life". The alchemist has discovered within himself the source from which his life comes forth. This fountain of life from which the water of life flows forth giving eternal youth. The source is singular, or one: the male and female are united. In alchemical images, we see a fountain from which two streams of water flow into one basin. Yet, it is only the discovery of this source, he has not yet partaken or fully understood its implications or experienced its true effects.

Being deep in Nigredo, when the white light appears, often the suddenness or brightness of Albedo can overwhelm and make it appear that everything is now better; obstacles have been overcome and wisdom has been gained. While it is true that certain obstacles have been overcome and knowledge gained, the wisdom and experience to apply it in everyday life is generally yet to be acquired. Thus, the stage of Albedo can sometimes be deceiving, at least in that respect, and care should be taken to keep that in mind. Just because the light is now shining, a plan has been made and the details of the surroundings illuminated, the person is still at the bottom of the well, steps must be taken to get out of the predicament in which he finds himself.

Until those steps are taken and completed, it may end up being a form of self-deception. Having a plan and executing a plan are two very different things, and just because one has come up with a great plan, does not get them out of the well. Those steps are yet to be taken, yet to be executed and until then it remains just a plan, no matter how detailed or marvelous it might be.

Albedo is the discovery of the hermaphroditic nature of oneself. In the spiritual sense, each person is a hermaphrodite. Each person contains the energies of the masculine and the feminine. The discovery of these energies is very much the phase of Albedo, however understanding their integration and balancing and bringing them together is much more the phase of Rubedo. Learning to balance and integrate these energies is a large part of the process of alchemy. It is very dualistic in nature, recognizing the masculine, recognizing the feminine, and once they are recognized and understood, integrating them into one balanced and whole being. This is also very emblematic of the Kabbalah with the Pillar of Severity, the Pillar of Mercy and the balanced Middle Pillar of Mildness.

We also see this in the embryonic phase of a fetus. There is no determinable gender until a certain number of weeks after conception when a certain hormone is delivered and the fetus now becomes inherently male or female. To use an eastern image, think of the Yin/Yang symbol. Within the feminine (the black or yin) portion of the image is imbedded a small amount of masculine energy; likewise, within the masculine (the white or yang) portion lies a small amount of the feminine. In this way, we see that the seemingly contradictory or opposing forces are actually complementary of one another as well as being interconnected in unexpected ways. The way that these energies intertwine, interact and balance one another forms a dynamic force of single purpose, of wholeness, which is the goal or end result when attempting to work with and balance these energies within oneself.

When we descend into this physical world, we enter a world of duality. On a physical/body/Salt level this may be expressed by the physical sexuality of the individual. However, our spirit, or Sulphur, remains androgynous, containing this duality within ourselves as well as the unity of both. This unity is not bound to space, time or matter, and achieving a balance that connects us back to this unification of the masculine and feminine energies is of great importance spiritually. Duality is an expression of unity in our physical world. It is temporal and will eventually cease to exist. When we are able to unite these energies, we then gain the ability to experience our true self. The conscious and unconscious, the masculine and the feminine, the internal and the external, the seen and the unseen have become totally united.

The phase of Albedo occurs when the Sun rises at midnight. It is a symbolic expression for the rising of the light at the very depths of darkness. The expression of Albedo arising from the dark depths of Nigredo. It is the time of the birth of Christ or Dionysus in the middle of the winter. It is the 'bright idea' out of nowhere, the proverbial light bulb going on, signifying that we have 'seen the light'.

Other common alchemical images for Albedo are baptism and the white dove, both of which happen to be derived from Christianity[5]. Baptism symbolizes the purification of both body and soul by 'living water'. 'Living water' is one way of viewing the creative force of the divine. It is the 'Life giving force of Creativity' (often associated to the element of Water), thus this Life force of Creativity may be known as 'Living Water'. Baptism allowed the purified soul to bring forth the resurrection of Christ within oneself. When referring to 'Christ', we are often referring to a specific state of consciousness, and not the man who is said to have lived around 2,000 years ago. Thus, it is symbolic of a conscious state of being, and represents our own inner divine essence.

Other symbols related to the phase of Albedo are: the white swan; the rose; and the image of the White Queen are but a few. Just as Lead is the metal of Nigredo, so is Silver is the metal of Albedo, having been transmuted from the Lead. As silver is the metal and color of the moon, the moon was often used as a symbol for Albedo.

---

[5] Many of the Alchemy texts and plates that we have come from Europe during the middle ages. As Christianity was the dominant religion of that time and location, many alchemical terms and ideas became couched in the familiar symbolism of the age. It was one way to avoid being burned at the stake or tortured, and thus a form of self-preservation.

Frater M.T.O.

This page intentionally left blank.

Here we see the White Queen holding two torches in the form of the magician, signifying "As Above, So Below". The torch below is touching the Earth of Nigredo, while the torch above is applying the flame to the retort, out of which is the Moon coming forth, emblematic of the Whitening aspect of Albedo.

She also stands upon the tetrahedron of Earth or Nigredo, indicating that she has passed through its phase, and now stands elevated above its challenges. But, the tetrahedron requires balance, upon which to stand. If not careful, she can topple over, back down to Nigredo. We also see Hermes, or Mercury, applying the flame of the spirit to the retort. Mercury too is touching the Earth, indicating the coming forth from Nigredo.

Thus, the flame of the Salt, or the Earth, and the flame of Mercury, or the spirit, are combining to bring forth the essence, or Sulphur, in this phase. Above the Moon, we see the Sun also depicted, emblematic of the coming phase of the perfection of the three principles and the individual, symbolizing the dual nature of existence.

Figure 2.2-Alchemical Plate representing the phase of Albedo

Citrinitas

Citrinitas, or the yellowing, is part of the transition from Albedo to Rubedo. In some schools of alchemy, Citrinitas is often omitted from the alchemical phases. Many have chosen to either eliminate this phase completely, or to simply combine it with that of Rubedo. This is unfortunate, as Citrinitas as its own separate phase is extremely valuable and of great importance in the work of the alchemist. It is a critical component in the process of spiritual alchemy, even if it is not a focus in the practical portion of the work. In herbal alchemy, we typically do not use Citrinitas in the physical portion of the work. Often, a 'new growth' within an herbal material to be ingested signifies something unwanted that has grown within the material. However, from a perspective of spiritual growth, Citrinitas is of critical importance. It represents the dawning of the solar light, in which the material just begins to move away from the reflective lunar light. It is the 'yellowing' part of the transformative change, and in ancient alchemy was also symbolic of the actual change from Silver into Gold. Here the substance may begin to putrefy slightly again, as it changes form, symbolizing the change from the Lunar to the Solar. Citrinitas stands for the dawning of the "solar light" inherent in one's being, and that the reflective "Lunar Light" was no longer necessary.

Just as with the approaching dawn, before the sun rises, the light of the Moon is unnecessary, as the light of the Sun precedes its arrival. Such it is with Citrinitas. Originally the transition from Albedo to Rubedo was accomplished via Citrinitas, but this was later often omitted. The red and white (Rubedo and Albedo) are the King and Queen who, at this stage, celebrate their "chemical wedding."

Many authors after the 15th century tended to suppress, or rather compress Citrinitas into the last stage of Rubedo. While the Albedo represented the moon, or female aspects, Citrinitas referred to the sun, or male aspects. The union of male and female (the so-called 'chemical wedding') was often a symbol of the work. From their conjunction, the hermaphroditic offspring, or the Philosophical Mercury, was born.

In the Jungian archetypal schema, Nigredo is representative of the Shadow self; Albedo refers to the anima and animus of the self; Citrinitas is the wise old man (or woman) archetype; and Rubedo is the true Self archetype which has achieved wholeness.

Citrinitas represents the growing consciousness. Just as Albedo was the light at the end of the dark tunnel of Nigredo, Citrinitas represents the learning, growth, nurturing and maturity of that Light within oneself. The Light of illumination and enlightenment initially revealed only a glimpse of itself within the phase of Albedo. In the phase of Citrinitas, that light has now revealed itself fully, and the journey of enlightenment now begins in earnest. The true work can now begin in the complete light of the morning sun.

As previously stated, many alchemists and even entire schools of alchemy have eliminated or compressed Citrinitas into the phase of Rubedo. However, it is a very important phase in the alchemical process, especially one in which a fermentation has been set to occur. Because it is one of the traditional four phases, it should be recognized and kept separate from the others. Think about life experiences. The phase of Citrinitas could be compared to the late teens and early twenties, as they are a period of explosive growth not only in the life of an individual, but in the development and education of the body and mind.

Just as Citrinitas represents the growth of the material in the physical alchemy, or the growth of the mind and spirit in internal alchemy. Now consider what life would be like by removing the experiences from that period of life, or compressing them with the late twenties and early thirties. That time period is critical to the development of each person as human beings, and in the same manner, so is Citrinitas critical to the development of the aspiring alchemist and his work, and it is valuable to consider them separately.

After being dumped into the 'well' of Nigredo, and then seeing the light above, illuminating the path and showing us the way out, Citrinitas represents the new growth, the steps to be taken to get out. As the climb begins, there are stones, crevices, nooks and crannies to be used for hand and foot holds, and the person can see each move in succession. Attempting this climb in the darkness could be treacherous and possibly deadly were one to slip and fall, but in the light of Albedo, it becomes a process, step by step, of slow and steady progress to climb and pull oneself out of the well. There may be an occasional slip, misstep or fall, but with perseverance and dedication, it is possible to make the climb.

This climb represents the new growth, the movement in the direction needed for true change to occur. Once the climb is completed, and the last step is taken, at last we stand on the brink of the well, looking back over the path we have traversed. New growth has occurred, and we may feel triumphant! However, one small misstep, perhaps even as we turn to walk away, thinking our journey complete, a small bit of ground may give way beneath our feet, making it possible for us to slip right back down into the well. After all that meticulous thought, planning and work to climb out, we sometimes find ourselves right back where we started, or at least having a bit of a setback. Care must be taken, for while the new growth and learning has taken place, knowledge obtained, there are still dangers and pitfalls which can prohibit our progress. We have made tremendous progress, but dangers still remain.

In alchemy, one should pay attention and keep a close watch out for this phase. It represents the achievement and acquisition of true knowledge and experience, and while it is not yet the phase of Rubedo, it stands just upon the precipice. Often in an alchemical experiment, as one watches over it closely, there is that moment, when the material teeters in between, almost achieving Rubedo, but something more yet needs to happen. Often in spiritual life, it is the same, we teeter on the brink of a breakthrough, having the knowledge, wisdom and experience, but just needing that one small thing to push us over the edge. Sometimes that push is a push forward, advancing us to true enlightenment and wisdom, but sometimes it may be a push backwards, sending us tumbling back into the abyss. This is the phase of Citrinitas.

The Peacock's Tail

While the Peacock's tail is not a phase of its own, due to the vast array of colors, it is often considered part of (or occurring during the phase of) Citrinitas. 'Cauda Pavonis', the peacock's tail, or the peacock itself, is a phase in which many colors may appear. Many alchemists place this phase before the phase of Albedo, the whitening, although some of them place it after. Gerhard Dorn, a 16th century alchemist said, "This bird flies during the night without wings. By the first heavenly dew, after an uninterrupted process of cooking, ascending and descending, it first takes the shape of a raven's head, then of a peacock's tail; its feathers becoming very white and good smelling, and finally becoming fiery red, indicating its fiery character." These colors refer to the three stages of the Great Work, with Rubedo, or redness, being the last.

The symbol of the peacock's tail was chosen because of the many colorful and brilliant 'eyes'. It is said that originally, they were the eyes of the Greek Argus, whose name means 'he who sees everything'. Argus was a very strong giant with a hundred eyes, of which always fifty were open and fifty were sleeping. He was decapitated by Hermes, and Hera, the mother goddess, placed his eyes on the tail of her favorite bird, the peacock.

The phase of the many colors was also symbolized by the rainbow, or the goddess of the rainbow: Iris, the messenger of the gods, especially between Zeus and the mortals.

The peacock's tail can have two meanings in the Great Work. Ironically, they are at the opposite ends of the spectrum of success. The first is that it represents the complete success of the work. It is the collection and totality of all colors within the white light. Remember, the white light refers to the second stage, albedo, or whiteness. In this sense the peacock was seen as a royal bird in ancient times, and it also corresponded with the phoenix.

The second meaning is that it represents the utter failure of the alchemical process. When the conscious enters the unconscious, "each part of a thought can take shape and become visible in color and form", according to a Chinese text about yoga exercises. One starts seeing all kinds of forms which look real and which look like they have an independent life. But one cannot go into it as it leads to discord of the mind, and possibly to schizophrenia. The alchemist is seeking unity, expressed in the white light.

It is known that during meditation exalted feelings and unusual observations can and do occur. In essence there are two kinds of observations. The first one is wanting to escape the discipline of meditation; which Zen practitioners call Makyo. Makyo are illusions we project onto reality to escape the guidelines of meditation. For example, the object of meditation is starting to radiate with a wonderful light or color, or it expands and contracts rhythmically. One starts to feel lighter or heavier, or one feels pleasant energies going through the body. All kinds of sensations can happen. Many meditators are readily distracted by these phenomena, and even take great interest in them, thereby neglecting the real purpose of their meditation. One needs to be aware of this.

A second cause of distraction is a change in consciousness whereby we look at the world in a different way than we did in the past. It can be quite a shock reverberating on the psychic or bodily level. The accompanying feelings can be quite wonderful. But the advice is: enjoy it, do not take it seriously, and continue with the meditation.

Figure 2.3-Alchemical Plate showing the Distillatio, or 'distillation'. At a certain point in the distillation the peacock's tail will appear.

Rubedo

Rubedo, or the reddening, is the final alchemical phase. Here the material in question has been wholly purified and now becomes the purified substance that has been sought. It is the purest of the pure, and is the continuation of the previous stages, representative of the pure and enlightened consciousness. It is the resurrection of Osiris and Christ, the consciousness of Krishna and Buddha, the true union of ourselves with the Divine spirit. Rubedo represents a level of enlightenment, when one has not only seen or been penetrated with the Divine light, but also maintains it within oneself in permanent residence. It certainly does not represent complete enlightenment (although it may), but more typically a certain a level of enlightenment and self-knowledge. When Rubedo has been realized, it represents an acceptance of one's spiritual inheritance and enlightenment, becoming greater than one was previously, having achieved a certain level of experience, knowledge, and wisdom.

Rubedo represents the ultimate triumph of the work, the completion of the Magnum Opus, the creation of the Philosopher's Stone in the form of a transparent red stone. This Stone, often portrayed as a Phoenix, was supposed to perfect anything from liquids to metals to human beings, bestowing healing, long life or immortality.

Albedo is a phase of which the meaning was kept secret for many centuries. The meaning of the last alchemical phase, Rubedo or redness, has been kept even more secret and is not easy to explain or understand, but rather typically must be experienced. Rubedo is the continuation of Albedo, which is why they are often seen connected to each other, like the White Queen and the Red King. Once the inner light has been discovered it must be made into the only reality in our consciousness. It is the merging of the two, the unification of the conscious mind (Albedo) and the unconscious mind (Rubedo). After having descended into the unconscious, into the darkness, into the underworld, we discovered the Light within ourselves, found that volatile spirit. Now the volatile spirit, or the quicksilver, must be fixated or coagulated. This means that our consciousness, or attentive mind, must completely penetrate our unconscious, or soul, everything that lay hidden within ourselves. By doing this we Coagulate, or recombine the two into a super-conscious state, taking the volatile (or the temporary) and making it durable (or lasting). When everything within ourselves has been purified and the Light appears, we must establish this Light and make it permanent so that it remains always present.

In Christianity, Rubedo corresponds with the resurrection of Christ. Jesus left behind the old body and brought his inner divine self, the Christ body, into his consciousness, and made it his own reality. What the Christ figure did two thousand years ago, each of us can do the same, because we are all sons and daughters of the divine, and we all carry the divine essence, or the Christ consciousness, within ourselves.

When Rubedo has been realized, the alchemist has accepted his spiritual inheritance. He has become what he always has been, but never realized he was. He has realized his divine essence while still in his physical body. It is the same as what the Gnostics called pneuma, the divine breath or spirit in each man that is concealed in the deep darkness of the world. When Rubedo has been manifested, the person is master over both the physical as the spiritual world. They have become a King and a Priest, a Queen and a Priestess, and have received their spiritual inheritance.

When the unification of all energies of the four aspects of totality has been achieved, a new state of being arises that is not nearly as susceptible to the winds of change. The state of enlightenment reached has lifted the alchemist to a higher level, to a level of a plateau where falling backwards, down the cliff, is no longer even a possibility. This is what is called the 'diamond body' which corresponds with the 'corpus incorruptible' (untouchable body) of

European alchemy. It is also the same as the 'corpus glorifications' (glorified body) referred to in the Christian tradition.

In yoga traditions, Rubedo corresponds with the unification of the spirit of man, called Atman, with Brahman. Atman is a part of Brahman. Brahman is the soul of the All, it is the breath or the energy flowing through you and giving life and consciousness. Atman is the individual self; Brahman is the universal self.

In our Well analogy, in Rubedo, we have not only escaped from the depths of the well, but we are physically miles and miles away from it. If we were sitting on the edge of the well, dangling our feet into its depths, taunting fate if we were to fall again, we would still be in Citrinitas. There is still that potential of falling into the well. Once the state of Rubedo is truly attained, we are likely not only miles away, but the well has now been filled in with rock and concrete, and we are now doing a TV interview on our travails inside of the well in a different city or state. There is no possibility of falling into that particular well again. It is a permanent escape without the possibility of a relapse or repeat. The person can now reflect upon their travail, see what was learned from the experience and can move ahead, as a changed and more enlightened individual…at least until the next (and a different) well is encountered.

The 'Corpus Hermeticum', written in 1460 says, "Ascend above any height, descend further than any depth; receive all sensory impressions of the created: water, fire, dryness and wetness. Think that you are present everywhere: in the sea, on earth and in heaven; think that you were never born and that you are still in the embryonic state: young and old, dead and in the hereafter. Understand everything at the same time: time, place, things: quality and quantity."

The union of the Red King with the White Queen, symbolic of the union of male-female, albedo-rubedo. In other words, when after having attained albedo (having discovered the divine light in oneself), the 'spirit' must be fixated (the descending eagle), resulting in Rubedo. The two lions with one head signifies the unified nature that has been attained. Out of its mouth flows the water of life.

Figure 2.4-Alchemical Plate showing the phase of Rubedo

This page intentionally left blank.

CHAPTER 4:
THE THREE PRINCIPLES OR
THE PRINCIPLE ELEMENTS
OF ALCHEMY

Having covered the phases of alchemy, or the 'place' of the game, we now will examine the principles of alchemy, or the game pieces. These pawns represent the substance being transformed, and can be acted upon as a whole, or broken into its respective pieces, or any combination of them. The three principles are Salt, Sulphur and Mercury, and correspond to the body, mind and spirit respectively. As an example of each of these principles, the creation of a Spagyric or herbal tincture will be used to explain how these principles work together, as well as work within the human body for healing. However, this information applies across the different types of alchemical work, whether herbal, mineral, metallic, animal or magical, the material is used in much the same way, but for this analogy we will use the creation of an alchemical herbal tincture.

Salt

Salt is one of the three elements in the trinity of substances in the Great Work of alchemy. Salt provides the physical body of the substance and the matrix wherein the alchemical Sulphur and Mercury can act. Mercury represents the watery aspect and sulfur is the fiery aspect, so is salt the form aspect in that salt is a crystalline form, or that of crystallized energy. So, it is also a name for the 'prima materia' or first matter itself, the stone of the philosophers. The alchemists say that in its lower aspect salt is 'bitter'. In this case, the salt is symbolic for knowledge and wisdom. Self-knowledge is often bitter and painful. Everyone has had to 'learn lessons the hard way' or has experienced a 'bitter realization', and these are all references to the bitterness of Salt. Sometimes they speak of the bitter 'sea water'. As water or the sea stands for the soul, it is a reference to the same self-knowledge, but often referencing learning a deeper internal or emotional lesson, rather than one in the physical world.

Salt is also seen as a symbol for the second phase of the Great Work, For the phase of Albedo, or the whitening, because here light breaks through in the form of wisdom. Christ is called 'Sal Sapientiae', the Salt of Wisdom' and he himself also said to his followers, "Ye are the Salt of the Earth". In the beginning of the Great Work, the salt is called impure. In that case, it equals the earth, the body, our everyday consciousness or being. The impure salt is to be dissolved into the divine water by which it is purified. In the phase of albedo salt arises as a purer form and is fixated, that is, it is crystallized into a pure salt.

Salt is the crystallization, the manifestation, the vehicle through which the subtler principles of Sulphur and Mercury work. Each principle is progressed through varying levels of density, with salt being the densest. It is composed of the Water and Earth elements.

Salt in the human form is reflected as the physical body, and is thus is very, very complex. There are literally billions and billions[6] of chemical reactions occurring in the body each second, many of which we know little to nothing about. The human body is one of the most beautiful mysteries we may ever come to know, a true microcosm of the greater external universe. The body is the anchor for our soul with the spirit giving it life; it is the temple in which they reside, at least for a time. Some of the ancient alchemists and kabbalists believed that the Salt, or body, facilitated the process of learning and knowledge, through physical sensation and experience, thus allowing that knowledge to transfer to the Sulphur, or soul, all of which is animated and given purpose by the Mercury or spirit.

In botanical kingdom, the Salt principle is reflected in the mineral matrix and physical makeup of the plant. As with the human, these minerals are the vehicle through which the Sulfur (essential oil) and the Mercury (alcohol/water soluble) principles work.

It should be noted that the term 'Salt' may refer to the actual mineral sodium, natron or some other of its many incarnations, but often it merely refers to whatever the physical substance is that is being transformed. Thus, if a tincture of Lemon Balm is being made, the leaves of the Lemon Balm are the 'Salts'. Likewise, if working with an Amethyst crystal, the physical amethyst is the 'Salt'. If working with Lead to transmute it into Gold, the Lead itself becomes the 'Salt'. This can sometimes be confusing, but any physical substance being used is alchemically a 'Salt'.

---

[6] To give an idea of how big the number is, just to stay alive, a human cell has to consume and replace all of its ATP (energy source) about once every one or two minutes. So that's about 10^7 chemical reactions (a 1 with seven zeros) each second. Multiply that by 86,400 (8.64×10^5) seconds per day. That's 8.64×10^{12} reactions per cell per day. Next, multiply that by 100 to 200 trillion cells in the human body (depending on how big you are), let's call that 100-trillion = 10^{14}. That comes to about 8.64×10^{26} chemical reactions per day. Next time someone asks "are you busy?", you can say "heck yes!"

As far as botanical extracts go, in Spagyrics we will work with these three principles through the various methods and preparations. Each principle of a plant is separated and purified, and then the three are reunited. This is the principle behind Spagery—to separate and recombine, thus following the great alchemical axiom, 'Solve et Coagula'.

For example, many conventional herbal tinctures, particularly those purchased commercially at retail, grocery and even natural food stores, will contain only the Sulfur (or oil) components of a plant, typically extracted with alcohol, water, glycerin or some other type of solvent. The herb will be macerated in this liquid menstruum (or solvent) for a period, after which the liquid part will be filtered out and sold as a tincture, while the remaining solid plant material will be used for some other purpose or even discarded. Thus, a majority of these tinctures are missing a whole 1/3 of a plant's constituents. And, the constituent that is missing is the mineral or Salt body, which is the vehicle through which the other principles work and manifest their healing and other positive benefits. Without a vehicle of manifestation, the work of the body, mind and spirit is wasted.

Anytime we as humans do anything, it is manifested through our Salts, or in other words, manifested physically. Perhaps our spirit (Mercury) dictates that we help someone in need, and so our minds (Sulphur) come up with a plan, but we still must take physical action, be it to hand someone in need a few dollars, drive down to a homeless shelter and work in the kitchen or provide some other means of assistance, it is all manifested physically, through our own 'Salt'. Likewise, if a doctor wishes to remove a tumor, he has the desire and the knowledge to do so, but he must physically use a scalpel, forceps and other tools of his trade to perform the surgery. Otherwise, these things only remain 'good ideas' in our minds and never come to pass. The Salt is truly the vehicle and the means of action and manifestation.

The same is true of healing with plants, minerals, metals and all types of alchemical work; the Mercury and Sulphur of the material, which contains a majority of the healing benefits, pass on their healing through the Salts of the substance. The Salts are the vehicle of manifestation. Eliminating, or not including, the Salts in an herbal remedy creates a type of disembodied medicine, a hobbled cure, and one which will have difficulty in truly manifesting solid results and effects.

Sulphur

Within the human body, the Sulfur principle is reflected as what might be termed our soul. The soul under this definition is our own unique expression of the universal life force. It is our individuality, our true essential nature, our essence, our unique identity, the flame of our awareness. Sulfur is a harmony of the Air and Fire elements. In that way, it is moveable, penetrating, hot, and diffusive. The correlation with Air is that our soul is not limited to our body; it has the ability to leave the body through astral projection, dream travel, and visionary journeying.

Different traditions look on the 'soul' in different ways. For our purposes, we will consider the 'soul' to be the internal makeup of an individual. This would make it comprised of the emotions, intellect, memories, knowledge, feelings and overall personality of the individual. Just as the Salt represents the physical body, so the Sulphur may represent the astral/mental/emotional subtle bodies of the individual.

This can be better understood when looking at the Sulfur principle within plants, which is reflected in its volatile or essential oils. The essential oil of a plant is a reflection of its true or internal nature and essence. It is that plant's unique flavor and expression. When one smells an essential oil of Frankincense for example, you are connecting with that plant's unique identity; there is no other smell on the face of the planet that smells quite like it. Even similar plants in the same family, while sharing some similarities, are still very distinct and different in their fragrance. It is the dynamic expression of the life force within that particular plant. Like Fire and Air, the essential oils of a plant volatilize very easily (they disperse through the air) and they are often very heated and intense, so much so that they can irritate or even cause slight burns on the skin.

The essential oils are both the most concentrated and most etheric constituent of a plant. Essential oils are exactly this energy in the plant, carrying a refined and instant expression of everything that plant is best at, but able to affect us in a totally non-physical way, through scent. Reaching out to us through their aromas, plants achieve a nearly disembodied state in which they can integrate into our own eternal self and retrain our inner archetype to better and higher states of perfection.

Sulfur is the level of the soul, the eternal aspect of a being. Sulfur can be thought of as a blueprint for that being's nature, much like the blueprint of a building. The Sulfur determines the materials, arrangement, and structure of the being, which in turn, determine its purpose and use in the world. It holds in pristine form the perfected ideal of that organism as an inner template that orders the growth and life of the being. This is the work of the soul, to communicate something higher to us, and to hold that spark within us so that all our being is guided by it.

In the purest tradition of Spagyric work, there is a focus on the essential oils, while still purifying and including the body, or salts, and spirit, or Mercury, of the material. In other words, in Spagyrics, the body of the plant or herb is included in the natural medicine along with the other constituents. This allows the healing properties of the plant to enter us completely, and their effects to be integrated at all levels of our being so that the healing is available in our physical, emotional life and spiritual life. This is one of the unique gifts of

Spagyrics, its ability to target a specific level which is the source of the imbalance, while also re-balancing the entire being. Working with essential oils alone does not bring this integration of body, spirit, and soul.

Consider that everything we do in this world, we manifest through the physical. If we want to open a business, it may start with a drive and an idea, but the actual manifestation of it is physical. Likewise, a Spagyric tincture also manifests its benefits through the Salts. However, if the physical constituent of the plant is missing, then a large part of the means by which it can manifest its properties is also missing. Therefore, the purified Salts of the plant are always included in an alchemical or Spagyric tincture, as it gives the vehicle for manifesting the healing benefits of the tincture (no matter whether those healing benefits are physical, mental or spiritual). This is the physical vehicle through which results are manifested, the philosophical Salt of the herb.

Mercury ☿

In Greek mythology, Mercury was the messenger of the gods, and was in constant movement between the above and the below, the world of the gods and the world of man. Within the human body, Mercury is the spirit, the animating life force. Whereas Sulfur is the soul, or the consciousness of the individual, Mercury is the life force that connects the soul (the above) to the body (the below) and gives it life. As the mediator between the two, it brings the soul down into the physical world.

Within the botanical kingdom, the Mercury is reflected in the alcohol and water-soluble constituents of the plant, called secondary metabolites in pharmacognosy (or plant/animal medicines). Every single plant found on our planet, when decomposed and fermented, will produce a form of ethyl alcohol. Ethyl alcohol, or Ethanol, is a byproduct of the metabolic process of sugars by yeast. As such, ethanol will be present in any yeast habitat. Ethanol is most commonly found in overripe fruits.

In alchemy, this operation of fermentation/decomposition is considered a type of death (via the alchemical process of Putrefaction), and it will yield ethyl alcohol. Thus, when a plant is put through a sort of death experience, and begins the process of decomposition, it 'releases' this alcohol, and the spirit is thus set free. This is incidentally, why alcoholic drinks are commonly called 'spirits'. The ancients noticed that alcohol was produced when a plant died and decomposed, so it was giving up its 'spirit'. So, the spirit of the plant is the alcohol and water components of the plant, yielded after its death. This is highly Mercurial in nature because alcohol tends to extract more volatile (Air) constituents (resins, essential oils) and water tends to extract more fixed (Water) constituents (polysaccharides, glycosides, alkaloids). Thus, the spirit, or Mercury of a plant brings together or harmonizes the two sides of the spectrum of botanical constituents.

Chemical Mercury is a very interesting substance itself. It is the only metal that is liquid in natural form, and it is highly moveable, changeable, and volatile, that is it turns to vapor (Air) very quickly. It is solid, yet also liquid at the same time, and can also convert into a gaseous form.

Philosophical Mercury is the principle of action, life, change, and balance. Like Mercury the deity, who travels between the worlds, Mercury the principle is a mediator. The Mercury level of being resides between the physical Salt body and the eternal Sulfur soul, and it both fixes the soul in a container of being and enlivens the body with the divine spark.

In plants, the Mercury resides in the alcohol, the spirit within the spirits. Like Mercury himself, alcohol travels between and links both poles of the journey: alcohol is both the product of the breakdown of one plant and is also used as the means to break down another, as in the creation of a Spagyric or alchemical tincture.

Chemically, alcohol is crucial to herbalism and Spagyrics, as it is both an extraction mechanism as well as a preservative, and it is typically far better at both these actions than its most-used substitute, glycerin. However, in Spagyric work, the subtle levels of being are of equal importance, and without the actual spirits, there would be no true spirit. So, while it is possible to create plant tinctures without alcohol, using glycerin, vinegar and other substitutes, the results are not true alchemical Spagyrics, as they are missing the true life-giving spirit found within alcohol.

Alcohol carries the Mercurial life force of the plant from its original being in Nature to your being as you ingest it, it is the reason that immediate effects are felt when taking Spagyric tinctures, long before any chemical physiological changes take place.

Mercury is the life force aspect and is carried in the alcohol of plants. Grapes due to their high natural sugar contents are more easily able to naturally ferment than many other plants, and as such grapes are often considered the highest of the plant kingdom. In fact, one alchemical saying is "all plants aspire to be grapes". This is why we use the 'Fruit of the Vine' in our alcohol for our tinctures. While it is possible to use grain alcohol, the fruit of the vine yields much better results in Spagyric work.

Brandy (which is essentially distilled Wine) is the preferred menstruum or solvent solution for creating alchemical or Spagyric tinctures. While vodka, everclear and other grain-based alcohol's can be used, they are not true fruits of the vine, and thus are considered a lesser substance, at least from a spiritual standpoint.

This page intentionally left blank.

CHAPTER 5:
THE SEVEN TRADITIONAL
PROCESSES OF ALCHEMY

Finally, we come to the processes in alchemy. The processes are various methods of performing or enacting change upon the object of the alchemical experiments. These processes are fundamental to the process of change that is to be undertaken and affected both upon the object as well as upon the alchemist. These changes lead us to the discovery of the Stone of the Philosophers, to true alchemical change and the discovery of the true nature of ourselves.

In the game analogy, the processes are the plays or the moves that may be made on our game board (the Phases), using the pieces or pawns (the principles). Each of the seven primary processes that we will delve into for this workbook will be explained. The number seven has always has a mystical connotation. There are 7 classic planets; 7 primary colors in a rainbow; the earth was supposedly created in 7 days; and we have 7 days in a week. These seven processes can certainly relate to each of these labels, and these connections or attributions are certainly something to be explored.

Calcination

Calcination is the first of the seven major operations in the alchemy of transformation. Externally, Calcination involves heating a substance to the point that it is reduced to a liquid or to ashes, or at least until it is fundamentally changed in substance, appearance and makeup. Internally, it represents a destruction of a part of the ego or an attachment to a material possession, habit or other part of our character that we wish to change or improve, beginning to turn the leaden part of our natures into gold. Physically, the Calcination process involves heating a substance in a crucible or over an open flame until it is changed in form. Chemically, Calcination is represented by sulfuric acid, which the alchemists made from a naturally occurring substance called Vitriol. Sulfuric acid is a powerful corrosive that eats away flesh and reacts with all metals except gold.

Psychologically, it is the destruction of a part of the ego, and our attachments to something material, be it a habit, possession or personality trait. Calcination is usually a natural humbling process as we are gradually assaulted and overcome by the trials and tribulations of life, though it can be a deliberate surrender of our inherent hubris gained through a variety of spiritual disciplines that ignite the fire of introspection and self-evaluation. Physiologically, the Fire of Calcination can be experienced as the metabolic discipline or aerobic activity that tunes the body, burning off excesses from overindulgence and producing a lean, mean, fighting machine. Calcination begins in the Base or Lead Chakra at the sacral cup at the base of the spine.

Figure 4.1-Placing the alchemist into the fires of Calcination.

Dissolution

Dissolution is the second major operation in the alchemy of transformation. Externally, Dissolution is the dissolving of the substance of the Calcination into a liquid solvent or menstruum. Internally, it is a further breakdown of the ego by immersion of the conscious into the unconscious mind. This allows the conscious mind to let go of its control, integrating new habits or behaviors, thus allowing the substance, or change, to materialize in the unconscious mind. It can represent the opening of energy channels in the body, to recharge and elevate the body.

In Spagyrics, Dissolution is the dissolving of the ashes from Calcination into pure water. Chemically, Dissolution is represented by iron oxide or rust, which illustrated the potentially corrosive powers of Water on even the hardest of metals. When processed, Vitriol breaks down into sulfuric acid and iron oxide, which are the first two arcana or secret ingredients. The Egyptians smelted Iron as far back as 1500 BCE and used iron compounds in various tonics and as disinfectants.

Psychologically, this represents a further breaking down of the artificial structures of the psyche by total immersion in the unconscious, non-rational part of our minds. It is, for the most part, an unconscious process in which our conscious minds let go of control to allow the surfacing of buried material. It is opening the floodgates and generating new energy from the waters held back. Dissolution can be experienced as "flow," the bliss of being well-used and actively engaged in creative acts without traditional prejudices, personal hang-ups, or established hierarchy getting in the way.

Physiologically, Dissolution is the continuance of the kundalini experience, the opening-up of energy channels in the body to recharge and elevate every single cell. Dissolution takes place in the Genital or Tin Chakra and involves the lungs and spleen.

Figure 4.2-Immersing the material into the Waters of Dissolution

Separation

Separation is the third operation of transformation in alchemy. Externally, Separation is the isolation of the components from the Dissolution via a filtration, and then discarding any unworthy material. Internally, it is the rediscovery of our essence, and reclaiming of our dreams and visions. It is a conscious process in which we analyze the formerly hidden material, the material that had been dissolved, and decide what to discard and what to keep and reintegrate into ourselves.

Chemically, Separation is represented by the compound sodium carbonate, which separates out of water and appears as white soda ash on dry lake-beds. The oldest known deposits are in Egypt. The alchemists sometimes referred to this compound as Natron, which meant the common tendency in all salts to form solid bodies or precipitates.

Psychologically, this process is the rediscovery of our inner and true essence and the reclaiming of dream and visionary "gold" previously rejected by the rational part of our minds. It is, for the most part, a conscious process in which we review formerly hidden material and decide what to discard and what to reintegrate into our refined personality. Much of this shadowy material are things we are ashamed of or were taught to hide away by our parents, churches, and schooling. Separation is letting go of the self-inflicted restraints to our true nature, so we can shine through.

Physiologically, Separation is following and controlling the breath in the body as it works with the forces of spirit and soul to give birth to new energy and physical renewal. Separation begins in the Navel or Iron Chakra located at the level of the solar plexus.

Figure 4.3-The alchemist preparing to perform a separation upon the material.

Conjunction

Conjunction is the fourth of the seven operations of alchemy. Externally, Conjunction is the recombination of the elements from the previous separation into a new and more pure substance. Internally, it is the bringing forth of our true nature, a union of the feminine and masculine parts of our nature into a heightened state of consciousness. It may also represent the combining of the conscious and unconscious parts of the mind, freeing our true selves from the constraints and preconceived notions of moral and social beliefs.

Conjunction is the recombination of the elements from the Separation, after they have been transformed by other processes (such as Calcination and Dissolution) into a new substance. Chemically it is symbolized by a nitrate compound known as cubic-saltpeter or potassium nitrate, which the alchemists called Natron or simply Salt. Blue-colored Natron acid, (aqua fortis), was made by mixing potassium nitrate with sulfuric acid and was used to separate silver from gold.

Psychologically, it is empowerment of our true selves, the union of both the masculine and feminine sides of our personalities into a new belief system or an intuitive state of consciousness. The alchemists referred to it as the Lesser Stone, and after it is achieved, the adept can clearly discern what needs to be done to achieve lasting enlightenment, which is union with the Over self. Often, synchronicities begin to occur that confirm the alchemist is on the right track.

Physiologically, Conjunction is using the body's sexual energies for personal transformation. Conjunction takes place in the body at the level of the Heart or Copper Chakra.

Figure 4.4-The conjunction (or joining) of the solar and lunar natures of the material.

Fermentation

Fermentation is the fifth operation in the alchemy of transformation. Externally, Fermentation is the chemical breakdown of a substance by bacteria, yeasts or other organisms. It is a two-step process, beginning with the putrefaction of the old substance, followed by the growth of the new substance. Internally, it is the spiritual light from above that reanimates, energizes and enlightens the new individual with new hopes and visions.

This two-step process begins with the Putrefaction of the hermaphroditic "child" from the Conjunction resulting in its death, pending a resurrection to a new level of being. The Fermentation phase then gives new life into the product of the Conjunction to strengthen it and ensure its survival.

Fermentation is the growth of a ferment (or a bacteria) in organic solutions, such as occurs in the fermenting of milk to produce curds and cheese or in the fermenting of grapes to make wine. Chemically, the process of Fermentation is represented by a compound called Liquor Hepatis, which is an oily, reddish-brown mixture of ammonia and the rotten-egg-smelling compound hydrogen sulfide. Egyptian alchemists made ammonia by heating camel dung in sealed containers and thought of it as a kind of refined Mercury that embodied the life force. Liquor Hepatis means "Liquor of the Liver," which they believed was the seat of the soul, and the color they associated with the compound was green, the color of bile. Surprisingly, Liquor Hepatis exudes a wonderful fragrance, and the alchemists made a perfume of it called "Balsam of the Soul."

Psychologically, the Fermentation process starts with the inspiration of spiritual power from Above that reanimates, energizes, and enlightens the alchemist. Out of the blackness of his Putrefaction comes the yellow Ferment, which appears like a golden wax flowing out of the foul matter of the soul. Its arrival is announced by a brilliant display of colors and meaningful visions called the

"Peacock's Tail." Fermentation can be achieved through various activities that include intense prayer, desire for mystical union, breakdown of the personality, transpersonal therapy, psychedelic drugs, and deep meditation. Fermentation is living inspiration from something that is or that exists totally beyond us or our world.

Physiologically, Fermentation is the rousing of living energy (chi or kundalini) in the body to heal and vivify. It is expressed as vibratory tones and spoken truths emerging from the Throat or Mercury Chakra.

Figure 4.5-The alchemist buries the solar and lunar natures, so that they may ferment in the soil and experience new growth into a new material.

Distillation

Distillation is the sixth major operation in the alchemy of transformation. Externally, Distillation is the boiling and condensing of the new fermented solution to increase its purity. Internally, it is the agitation and sublimation of the individual necessary to ensure that no impurities from the ego or id are incorporated into the final stage.

Distillation is the boiling and then condensation of the fermented solution to increase its purity, such as takes place in the distilling of wine to make brandy. Chemically, Distillation is represented by a compound known as Black Pulvis Solaris, which is made by mixing black antimony with purified sulfur. The two immediately clump together to make what the alchemists called a bezoar, a kind of sublimated solid that forms in the intestines and brain.

Psychologically, Distillation is the agitation and sublimation of psychic forces necessary to ensure that no impurities from the inflated ego or deeply submerged id are incorporated into the next and final stage. Personal Distillation consists of a variety of introspective techniques that raise the content of the psyche to the highest level possible, free from sentimentality and emotions, cut off even from one's personal identity. Distillation is the purification of the unborn Self.

Physiologically, Distillation is raising the life force repeatedly from the lower regions in the cauldron of the body to the brain (what Oriental alchemists called the Circulation of the Light), where it eventually becomes a wondrous solidifying light full of power. Distillation is said to culminate in the Third, Eye area of the forehead, at the level of the pituitary and pineal glands, in the Brow or Silver Chakra.

Figure 4.6-The material emerges, or is 'distilled', from the waters of fermentation.

Coagulation

Coagulation is the seventh and final operation of transformation in alchemy. Externally, Coagulation is the precipitation or sublimation of the purified ferment from distillation. It is, essentially, a final and glorified conjunction, bringing together the principles in one final moment of purity, thus creating the finished and elevated alchemical material. Internally, Coagulation incarnates and releases the Ultima Materia of the soul, creating a permanent vehicle of Consciousness that embodies the highest aspirations of the soul.

Chemically, Coagulation is represented by a compound called Red Pulvis Solaris, which is a reddish-orange powder of pure sulfur mixed with the therapeutic mercury compound, red mercuric oxide. The name Pulvis Solaris means "Powder of the Sun" and the alchemists believed it could instantly perfect any substance to which it was added.

Psychologically, Coagulation is first sensed as a new confidence that is beyond all things, though many experience it as a second body of golden coalesced light, a permanent vehicle of consciousness that embodies the highest aspirations and evolution of mind. Coagulation incarnates and releases the Ultima Materia of the soul, the Astral body, which the alchemists also referred to it as the Greater or Philosopher's Stone. Using this magical Stone, the alchemists believed they could exist on all levels of reality.

Physiologically, this stage is marked by the release of the elixir in the blood that rejuvenates the body into a perfect vessel of health. A brain ambrosia is said to be released through the interaction of light from the phallic-shaped pineal gland and matter from the vulva of the pituitary. This heavenly food or viaticum both nourishes and energizes the cells without any waste products being produced. These physiological and psychological processes create the second body, a body of solid light that emerges through the Crown or Gold Chakra.

In creating an Herbal alchemical tincture, your tincture releases a portion of this elixir into your bloodstream, in the form of its healing energies. There are many ways to gain these benefits and increase vitality, including creating the 7 planetary tinctures and stones, as well as the Red Tincture alluded to in the physiological effects above. The purpose of these phases, principles, processes and procedures is to gain enlightenment and life everlasting. Each of these steps takes us in that direction, and leads us to the final creation of the Quintessence, the Stone of the Philosophers: True Wisdom and Perfect Happiness, the Summum Bonum.

Figure 4.7-The coming together of the Red King and the White Queen, the Solar and Lunar natures.

This page intentionally left blank.

CHAPTER 6:
THE USE OF THE FOUR PHASES, THREE PRINCIPLES AND SEVEN PROCESSES WITHIN ALCHEMY

When practicing Alchemy, you will not always utilize all seven of the primary alchemical processes. Particularly in Herbal Alchemy, but also in the other types of alchemy, they are not all necessary depending upon the goal. For example, in Herbal Alchemy when creating a Spagyric or tincture, the phase of Fermentation is not only not used, it is typically not desired. Unless a food analyzation laboratory is available, it is not a good idea to consume any material that has fermented, as the end product may have unknown effects. When creating an artificial mineral stone, calcination is not used, but rather the rawer form of the Salts. At times, some processes that are used may be slight modifications or only portions of the actual full process.

Bear in mind that the 7 primary processes are just that, the primary ones. There are numerous processes that may be enacted upon a material, and found in Appendix A of this book, is a list of 109 possible alchemical processes. Just remember that while the primary processes each have their place, and accomplish something specific in the process, both physical to the material being worked with as well as spiritually within the alchemist, there are numerous other processes that may be used, and in other cases only a few may be used.

As an example, here is a summary of the processes that are used when creating a Spagyric or herbal tincture.

Conjunction is the first process used, as the solvent solution is added to the herbal salts to leech out the essential oils prior to any other operations.

Separation is used several times throughout the Spagyric process. First, after the herbal material and the alcohol have been combined, after having a chance to macerate for a few weeks, you will separate the remaining herbal material from the liquid menstruum solution. Next, you will separate the ash, removing the larger and impure particles from the purer ash substance. Finally, after mixing the filtered ash with the water, you will again filter or separate out the impure ash that does not dissolve properly.

Calcination is used mid-way through the process to calcinate and burn the herb, to chemically alter its substance, and to purify the material with fire.

Dissolution is used after the Calcination process to dissolve the purified ash into pure water, which continues to also chemically alter the substance as well as to purify it with water.

Conjunction is another process that you will use several times. Conjunction is the combining of two or more materials to create a new substance. One of your first acts will be performing a conjunction with your chosen herb and the alcohol. Then, you will also combine the purified ash with purified water, to cause yet another change to your herb.

While there will be no pure Fermentation, the process of fermentation is often seen as a two-fold process, putrefaction (or the breakdown of the material), followed by Fermentation (or the growth of the new material). When you grind your herb in a mortar and pestle at the very beginning, you are instituting a type of putrefaction, or breakdown of the material. While it doesn't fit the physical process exactly, it is metaphorically very similar. Also, when you combine your herb with the alcohol, that breakdown, or putrefaction, continues to break down the Salt of your herb, as it draws out the Sulphur, or essential oils.

It should be noted that a true fermentation with herbal tinctures that are to be ingested is likely NOT a good thing. If your herb has a growth of something new and unexpected (especially considering you are using alcohol as a menstruum), that growth should be considered a Cauda Pavonis (Peacock's Tail) and should be discarded. Without the capabilities of a full blown chemical laboratory, where detailed analysis can be conducted on the new growth, it is very possible that it may be dangerous to ingest. Should you see anything growing abnormally within your menstruum solution, you should not ingest it, but should either discard it, or perhaps keep it for further study.

Distillation is used towards the end of the process when you evaporate the purified water, and are left with the purified Salts of your herbal material. While this is not using a distillation apparatus, or other intricate vessels, it is nevertheless the concentrating the purified Salts from the purified water, which is, in essence, Distillation. Distillation may also be used after the finished product is completed, in order to concentrate the solution. However, this is often unnecessary, as the finished product is extremely potent due to the energy and alchemical processes already enacted upon it.

Finally, the final conjunction of the purified Salts and the menstruum solution (which contains the Sulphur and Mercury) is the Coagulation. The final combination of the three principles into a new substance, which takes on a life of its own and gives the benefits and healing of body, mind and spirit.

This page intentionally left blank.

SECTION 2: PRACTICAL APPLICATIONS

CHAPTER 7:
PREPARATION FOR
ALCHEMICAL WORK

As stated previously, alchemy is not a physical process, nor a mental one, nor a spiritual one, but rather it is a synthesis of all three. This means that while some small benefit may be gained solely by doing the physical work of alchemy, or that while some internal changes may be seen by simply performing meditations based upon alchemical work, or that some progress and level of understanding might be made simply by reading and assimilating the information presented in this book, the whole of all of these worked together is MUCH greater than the sum of its parts.

As you work with and connect physically, spiritually and energetically with the substance of your alchemical work, the changes enacted upon it in conjunction with the meditations performed will likely far exceed your expectations for change within yourself. Alchemy is a life-changing process, and one that is not just experienced once, but many times over! The process repeats itself again and again, as we continue to purify and enlighten ourselves, raising ourselves to a higher state of spiritual evolution, and becoming 'more' than human. It is of critical importance to read all the information in the first section of this book, and complete both the physical experiments and the processes listed here in conjunction with the meditations and internal work. Lastly it is extremely important to journal your work. Having a baseline to reflect upon later, as well as being able to see changes taking place within yourself is a critical component to alchemical, and really any form of spiritual work.

Alchemical Meditational Work – Entering the Alchemy Lab
A Note on Meditation

Options are given in this workbook to accommodate a range of experiences in meditations. These options vary between 5 and 20 minutes in length. If you are experienced at meditation, then 20 minutes is likely not going to be a huge challenge. Given a purpose, and a substance on which to focus, 20 minutes can fly by for those with experience at meditation. However, if you are new to a meditational practice, 20 minutes can not only seem like a lifetime, but it would probably be a waste of your time. If you are a beginner to meditation, that's GREAT! There are no problems if you are new to meditation, simply follow the instructions here and jump right in! It is a very useful skill, and one that you will improve upon just while working through this workbook. Trying to bench press 500 lbs. on your first day at the gym is not only setting you up for failure, it would likely cause physical damage as well. While there is no danger here in these basic meditations, trying to meditate for 10, 15 or 20 minutes when you are new to meditation is only setting you up for failure. Set a time that you feel you could accomplish (probably not less than 5 minutes though), and work on it. You'll find it becomes easier and easier as you practice. It may help, especially at first, to use some type of voice recorder (many cell phones have a recording function) to record the meditations, and use that to walk yourself through them. The point is not to worry too much about whether you've spent enough time, but focusing and spending quality time in meditation no matter how experienced you might be.

Week 1 Alchemical Meditation - Entering the Alchemy Lab

Meditation is not only a useful skill and practice to have, but it is healthy for the mind, body and spirit. During meditation, there are opportunities for us to learn and grow in many ways. Some of the goals in this type of meditation are purification, reconnection, restoration, and circulation of the life force throughout the vessel, the vessel in this case, being you. In other words, just as you might pour two different solutions into a jar, and then swirl them around to mix them, so it is with meditation. We are swirling around the energies, purifications, calcinations and other processes and practices, to enact and cause change within ourselves.

You should use this "Entering the Alchemy Lab" meditation (or some form thereof) any time before beginning your alchemical work. It is also advisable to use this meditation just prior to your weekly meditations, flowing directly out of this one and into your weekly meditation.

Reaching a true state of relaxation can be very difficult, especially for the beginner. In today's world, we are often so caught up in the hectic and rushed nature of everyday life, that it can be difficult for us to slow down and just have some quiet time to ourselves. This meditation of "Entering the Alchemy Lab" is one of progressive relaxation, and it may take you a few times to learn to achieve and maintain a relaxed state. It allows you to focus only on your breathing, and on one part of your body at a time. Its simple nature makes it easy to use, and it has great effects in preparing the mind, body and spirit for deeper states of meditation and contemplation.

If you wish to visualize your own personal alchemy lab,

complete with beakers, vessels, ovens, distillation apparatus and more, feel free to do so. However, such in-depth visualization skills and astral creation work are a bit beyond the scope of this book. However, instructions on doing so will be coming out in a future workbook.

Entering the Alchemy Lab

1. Begin by closing your eyes and becoming aware of your breathing. Take a deep breath in through the nose; allow your stomach to expand as you breathe in. Hold the breath for a few seconds and then breathe out your mouth slowly, allowing your body to completely relax on the out breath. Your stomach should contract as your breath out.

2. Take note of sounds that you may hear. It may be cars driving by, the shifting of your chair, children playing in another room, or dogs barking. Know that these sounds are around you, but they do not interfere with your meditative state.

3. Also, take note of the feelings about you. The chair on which you are sitting or the floor on which you are lying. The touch of your clothes upon your body, any breeze that may be passing by, touching you and leaving a sensation in its wake. Know that these feelings are around you, but that they also do not interfere with your meditative state.

4. Consciously slow your breathing down with each breath you take. Breathe in through your nose; hold it for a few seconds, and then exhale out your mouth and again hold for a few seconds. With each breath, you take your body is becoming more relaxed and your mind is becoming more clear and focused. Breathing in through your nose, holding it for a few seconds, and then exhaling out your mouth and holding for a few seconds. Your breathing is becoming measured, deep and rhythmic.

5. Now with each breath, begin to visualize a stream of white light travelling into the crown of your head. This energy travels down and throughout your entire body, and fills your body with this pure white light.

6. Breathe in the light through your nose and bring your awareness to your face. Allow any tension in your forehead, your eyes, and jaw to relax as you breathe out. Your face is now completely relaxed.

7. Again, breathe in the light through your nose and bring your awareness to your throat, neck and shoulders. As you breathe in, focus on any tension in your neck and throat and particularly your shoulders to release with the out breath.

8. Again, breathe in the light through your nose and see it travelling down each of your arms, all the way to your fingertips. Feel your

arms dropping, as they relax, being filled with this light, and any tightness or tension is dissipated as you exhale.

9. Again, breathe in the light; and as you do you see the light travelling around your chest and heart area. As the light swirls around your heart area, you feel a sense of warmth, comfort and love. Exhale deeply, allowing any tensions in your chest to dissolve and leave with the exhaled breath.

10. Again, breathe in the light and bring your awareness to your stomach. Allow your stomach to expand completely with light. As you breathe out, release any tension found in your stomach area.

11. Take a deep breath in through your nose, and as you do, see the light coming in and travelling down your spine. Your spine is filling with light, releasing any tension in the discs and joints as you breathe out.

12. Breathe in the Light and bring your awareness to your hips, dissolving any tension there, and as you exhale allow your hips to relax.

13. Again, breathe in the light and see the light travelling into your upper legs and thighs, releasing all tension and stress on the out breath. Any tension in your thighs is being released now.

14. Again, breathe in the light and bring your awareness to your lower legs. You see white light travelling into your knees and lower legs and releasing all tension and stiffness. Any tension in your calves is being released now as you exhale.

15. As you breathe in the Light again, bring your awareness to your feet. See the Light permeating your feet, from the instep to the sole, from the heels to the tips of your toes. Exhale and see and feel any tension in your feet being released on the out breath.

16. Now once again breathe in this Light and allow this beautiful light to go to any parts of your body that need healing. It could be a past injury or simply a weakness in your body that you are aware of. Simply allow the light to completely surround this part of your body now. Your entire body is now full of this beautiful white light.

17. And now the light expands into your aura. It expands beyond the physical boundaries of your body and permeates the energy field in your aura. See this light releasing any energy in your aura that needs to be released, that is not supporting you, filling in any

cracks or holes that may be present. See your physical body, your energy centers and your aura glowing with this divine healing energy. See your aura like an egg; very strong and free from holes and imbalances.

18. Your body is feeling very relaxed now. Your mind is clear and focused. Your emotions are feeling calm and content. Rest here a few moments…See yourself in your mind's eye entering your own personal alchemy lab. Walking through the door into your practical lab, ready to begin the work ahead.

19. It is now time to leave this meditation and move on. When you feel ready, gently bring your awareness back to your body, and to the room you are in. Hear once again the sounds around you, the feeling of the chair under you as you return to full consciousness. Give your fingers and toes a wiggle and gently open your eyes – coming back to waking consciousness.

This page intentionally left blank.

CHAPTER 8:
ALCHEMICAL JOURNALING

Journaling is a critical component of any type of magical, meditational or self-developmental work. It allows us to see where we've been, keeps details of lessons learned, insights gleaned and personal growth achieved. They can be short and sweet, long and wordy or anywhere in between. The important thing is that you write down SOMETHING about the experience that you just had. You should journal immediately after any work or experience, and it is also wise to leave at least a few lines to add a comment later regarding the experience, as oftentimes insights and additional knowledge or information will come our way after the fact.

For example, in creating an herbal tincture and working with your herb, perhaps in your meditation you will see a symbol. You should journal that symbol and describe as well as draw it. A few days or weeks later, perhaps you see that symbol and then you will understand WHY you had been shown it during your meditation. Leaving a few lines to add to your entry about the experience of seeing the symbol a few days later may be critical to reading and fully understanding that experience 3-4 years down the road.

When journaling, there are various patterns that you will come to notice over time. Some of those involve astrological timing, signs and their relationship to your own astrological natal chart. As such, in the journaling pages that follow is included places to record some basic information regarding the date, time, sun sign, moon sign and moon phase during the time when you performed the meditation. This information can come in handy down the road, when you begin comparing your varied and multiple alchemical works to one another. It is always interesting to find that you have the most insights during a waxing moon, or that your work is especially powerful when the Sun in is Aries. Following that information, are lined pages for you to journal your actual experiences.

Alchemical Journal - Entry 1

Name: _____ Date/Time: _____

Sun Sign: _____ Moon Sign: _____

Moon Phase: New / Waxing / Full / Waning / VoC

_____

_____

_____

_____

_____

_____

_____

_____

_____

_____

_____

_____

_____

_____

_____

_____

_____

_____

_____

_____

_____

_____

_____

_____

_____

Alchemical Journal - Entry 2

Name: _____ Date/Time: _____

Sun Sign: _____ Moon Sign: _____

Moon Phase: New / Waxing / Full / Waning / VoC

_____

_____

_____

_____

_____

_____

_____

_____

_____

_____

_____

_____

_____

_____

_____

_____

_____

_____

_____

_____

_____

_____

_____

Alchemical Journal - Entry 3

Name: _____ Date/Time: _____

Sun Sign: _____ Moon Sign: _____

Moon Phase: New / Waxing / Full / Waning / VoC

Alchemical Journal - Entry 4

Name: _____ Date/Time: _____

Sun Sign: _____ Moon Sign: _____

Moon Phase: New / Waxing / Full / Waning / VoC

Alchemical Journal - Entry 5

Name: _____ Date/Time: _____

Sun Sign: _____ Moon Sign: _____

Moon Phase: New / Waxing / Full / Waning / VoC

_____

_____

_____

_____

_____

_____

_____

_____

_____

_____

_____

_____

_____

_____

_____

_____

_____

_____

_____

_____

_____

_____

_____

_____

_____

_____

Alchemical Journal - Entry 6

Name: _____ Date/Time: _____

Sun Sign: _____ Moon Sign: _____

Moon Phase: New / Waxing / Full / Waning / VoC

_____

_____

_____

_____

_____

_____

_____

_____

_____

_____

_____

_____

_____

_____

_____

_____

_____

_____

_____

_____

_____

_____

_____

CHAPTER 9:
PURSUING THE STONE OF
THE PHILOSOPHERS

As stated previously, alchemy is both a metaphorical as well as a practical process of growth, transmutation and change. The information contained within this book covers the 4 primary phases, the 3 principle elements and the 7 fundamental processes used in certain schools of alchemy. In some schools, certain phases or processes are eliminated or added, although the 3 principles typically remain the same. For the purposes of this and future workbooks, the material contained herein will be the primary information and knowledge necessary to complete the workbooks, from both an external point of view, of working with a specific material, as well as an internal point of view, in working with yourself.

Every attempt has been made to make this material far easier to understand and comprehend than many ancient or traditional alchemical texts, which tend to use symbol and metaphor to the extreme with little to no explanation. While there is certainly a benefit and reason for doing so, making the art and science of Alchemy more accessible is the goal of this series of workbooks. Using analogies, such as the Well example for the phases and the Game analogy for all of the various elements of alchemy presented here, is one method of making the basic elements of alchemy easier to understand and comprehend.

Alchemy, like many spiritual pursuits, is truly a lifelong quest. It is a never-ending series of experiments and internal mystical work, which can lead to a fulfilling life, full of wonder and excitement. Learning about yourself is difficult, to be sure, but also can be truly wondrous and satisfying. Changing yourself is one of the more difficult things that you can and will ever do, and Alchemy provides one of the most detailed and observational methods of gauging the progress that you have made on this spiritual path.

Consider if you will a classic car, being restored over time by an aficionado. When he purchases it, it may be heavily used, rusted, worn out or even dilapidated in its appearance and functionality. Over time, however, he invests of himself in a labor of love (and, of course, no small amount of money!) in restoring the automobile to a pristine condition. Slowly, over time, the car begins to not even resemble its former appearance, but takes on a showroom like quality. At some point, the person takes a look at the photo album of their progress. Seeing the rust disappear, replaced by new metal; old paint sanded down and repainted with a shiny new coat; ripped and torn seats refinished and replaced, and so on. There is a very apparent progress and change taken upon as the car is restored to an immaculate appearance.

So it is with the process of Alchemical change within each of us. Slowly the rust of undesirable habits and behaviors is replaced by new and better ones; the old rough edges of ourselves is sanded down, and smoothed by the trials of self-discovery; the ripped and torn parts of ourselves on the inside are refinished and take on a new sense of purpose. Upon reflection, these things are very measurable and obvious, should we actually take the time and effort to invest in ourselves.

There are no shortcuts. Just as a quality house that might take a year to build, cannot be built in 2 months without defects in workmanship, poor materials or a combination of both, so quality work on ourselves cannot take shortcuts, unless we are willing to end up with a product of lower quality. Time and effort take discipline to adhere to and endurance to stick with the process. This can certainly be developed, but the desire and the will to undertake the journey must be present and strong.

One of the amazing things about alchemy is that there is no set dogma, no particular belief system. Providing that you can harmonize the spiritual practices found within alchemy with your particular belief system, the you can practice alchemy as an addition to your own spiritual practice, not necessarily a replacement of it. There are alchemical practitioners from numerous faiths around the world including Christian, Muslim, Buddhist, Sufi, Pagan and numerous other faiths. Alchemy as it is, is more a system of practice and self-spiritual development than one of belief in a particular dogma. This makes alchemy an amazing additional practice to many spiritual belief systems, and alchemy opens its doors to any who wish to undertake its quest.

As you embark upon your Alchemical journey, bear in mind that if you cheat or take shortcuts, the only one truly being cheated is yourself. If you choose to continue working within the Peacock Publishing series of workbooks, you will find alchemical work, both external and internal, designed to be easy to use, easy to understand while still carrying an amazing level of internal mystical and magical work and change to be enacted upon yourself, as well as the object and material of your alchemical work.

Should you apply yourself, put in the work and take upon yourself the labor of practical and spiritual alchemy, you will find not only a system of self-improvement, but one of spiritual, mystical and magical power. Your spirit, or body of light, will be strengthened and you will find yourself able to exert your will to affect the world around you. Your mind will be opened, and you will suddenly begin to see behind the systems of symbols that exist all around you, both ancient and modern. Your body will become strong, and through the partaking of the physical outcome of your alchemical work, your health and vitality will improve immensely. Alchemical work not only provides enlightenment and inner vision, but strengthens the entirety of the self, body, mind and spirit, into a new and improved version of the person who you used to be. This is the measured progress that can be easily and readily seen not only by yourself, but also by others who know you in the world around you.

The search for the Philosophers Stone has long been the Magnum Opus, or Great Work, of the ancient alchemists. As you now embark upon your journey, and become a true alchemist, may the blessings of deity, however you may envision that, be upon you. May your work be strong, your will powerful and your quest successful. Thus it begins for you, the true quest for your higher and true nature, to be found through the search for the quintessence, the Stone of the Wise, true wisdom and perfect happiness, the Summum Bonum.

APPENDIX A: GLOSSARY OF ALCHEMICAL PROCESSES

The following list of 109 Alchemical Processes was researched and written by renowned Alchemist Adam McLean. The original can be found on "The Alchemy Website" at http://www.alchemywebsite.com/alch-pro.html. They are presented and printed here with the author's full knowledge and permission.

1. Ablation
The separation of a component by removing the upper part, sometimes by skimming it off the surface or by wicking it up using a feather or cloth.

2. Albification
The making of the matter in the alchemical work become white.

3. Ablution
The purification of a substance by successive washings with a liquid.

4. Amalgamation
Formation of an amalgam, or alloy, of a metal with mercury. This term is sometimes extended to mean any union of metals.

5. Ascension
When the active or subtle part rises up in the flask, usually by heating.

6. Assation
The reduction of a substance to a dry ash by roasting.

7. Calcination
The breaking down of a substance by fierce heating and burning usually in an open crucible.

8. Cementation
Acting upon a substance by mixing it in layers with a powdered (often corrosive) material, such as lime. This mixture is then made to react and weld together by heating to a high temperature in a cementing furnace.

9. Ceration
The making of a substance to soften and appear like wax. This is often accomplished by continually adding a liquid and heating.

10. Cineration
The reduction of a substance to ashes by heating.

11. Circulation
The purification of a substance by a circular distillation in a pelican or closed distillation apparatus. Through heating the liquid component separates, is condensed and descends to the substance in the flask.

12. Coadunation
Another term for coagulation.

13. Coagulation
The conversion of a thin liquid into a solid mixture through some inner change, as with the curdling of milk. This can be accomplished by a variety of means - by the addition of a substance, by heating or cooling.

14. Coction
The cooking or heating of a substance at a moderate heat for an extended period.

15. Cohobation
The frequent removal of the moist component of a substance by heating. Often the moist component (or some other liquid) is added and the process continued.

16. Colliquation
The conjuction or melting together of two fusible substances.

17. Coloration
Tinging a substance by adding a dye or coloured tincture. Colouring can by either by tinging the whole body or by producing a surface coating.

18. Combustion
The burning of a sustance in the open air.

19. Comminution
The reduction of a substance into a powder, either by grinding, pulverising, or forcing it through a sieve.

20. Composition
The joining together of two different substances.

21. Conception
The marriage or union of the male and female aspects of substances.

22. Concoction
The cooking or heating of a mixture of substances at a moderate heat for an extended period.

23. Congelation
The conversion of a thin flowing liquid into a congealed thick substance, often by heating.

24. Conglutination
The conversion of a substance into a gluey mass, often by a putrefaction.

25. Conjunction
The joining of two opposite components, often seen as the union of the male and female, the subtle and gross, or even the elements.

26. Contrition
The reduction of a substance into powder only by means of fire.

27. Copulation
A conjunction, or joining of two opposite components, seen through the metaphor of the union of the male and female, or the union of the fixed and the volatile.

28. Corrosion

The eating up of a substance by an acid, alkali or corrosive material.

29. Cribation

The reduction of a substance to a powder by forcing through a sieve or mesh.

30. Crystallization

The formation of crystals out of a solution of the substance usually in water, either by their gradual formation from the liquid, or by evaporation of the liquid.

31. Dealbation

The making of the black substance of the alchemical process become brilliant white.

32. Decoction

The digestion of a substance in the flask without the addition of any other material.

33. Decrepitation

The crackling and splitting apart of substances, for example common salt, on heating.

34. Deliquium

The reduction of a solid placed in a damp place to a liquid by its absorbing water from the air.

35. Descension

When the subtle or active part of a substance is made to go down to the bottom of a flask, rather than ascend as a vapour.

36. Dessication

The drying or removal of all the moisture in a substance.

37. Detonation

The explosive burning of substances on heating, for example substances mixed with nitre.

38. Digestion
The slow modification of a substance by means of a gentle heat.

39. Disintegration
The breaking down or dissociation of a substance into different parts.

40. Dispoliaration
The dissolving or transforming of a dead substance into a liquid.

41. Dissociation
The breaking down or disintegration of a substance into different parts.

42. Dissolution
The dissolving or transforming of a substance into a liquid.

43. Distillation
The separation of a volatile component from a substance by heating so as to drive off the component as a vapour which is condensed and collected in a cooler part of the apparatus.

44. Divapouration
An exhalation of dry vapours from a substance, which can occur at different degrees of heat.

45. Division
The separation of a substance into its elements.

46. Ebullition
An effervescence produced through fermentation.

47. Edulceration
The washing of a salty substance till all the salts are removed.

48. Elaboration
The general term for the process of separating the pure from the impure, and leading a sustance towards perfection, which can be done through a variety of means and processes.

49. Elevation
The raising of the subtle parts of a substance upwards, away from the bodily residues, into the upper parts of the vessel.

50. Elixeration
The conversion of a substance into an elixir.

51. Evaporation
The removal of the watery part of a substance by gentle heating, or being left a long time in a dry place.

52. Exaltation
An operation by which a substance is raised into a purer and more perfect nature.

53. Exhalation
The release of a gas or air from a substance.

54. Expression
Extraction of juices by means of a press.

55. Extraction
The preparation of the subtler and purer parts of a substance, usually by macerating it in alcohol. The extract can then be separated from the residue.

56. Fermentation
The rotting of a substance, usually of an organic nature, often accompanied by the release of gas bubbles.

57. Filtration
The process or removing the grosser parts of a substance by passing through a strainer, filter or cloth.

58. Fixation
The make a volatile subject fixed or solid, so that it remains permanently unaffected by fire.

59. Foliation

The making some substances puff up in layers, like leaves lying on top of one another, usually undertaken by heating.

60. Fulmination

The preparation of a fulminate or explosively unstable form of a metal. Sometimes applied to any process in which a sudden eruptive event occurs.

61. Fumigation

The alteration of a substance by exposing it to a corroding smoke.

62. Fusion

The joining of powdered substances together, or the conversion of a substance into a new form, by means of an extremely high degree of heat, sometimes using a flux.

63. Glutination

Turning a substance into a gluey, glutinous mass.

64. Gradation

The gradual purification of a substance, often through a series of stages.

65. Granulation

The reduction of a substance to grains or powder. There are various means of doing this - pounding, grinding, using thermal shock by heating and rapid cooling, and many others.

66. Grinding

The reduction of substances to a powder, usually through the use of a mortar and pestle.

67. Humectation

A process by which humidity is given to the substance, usually not by the direct addition of liquid, but by a gradual process of absorbing moisture.

68. Ignition
The self-calcination of a substance by it burning itself in a crucible.

69. Imbibition
The feeding of a process by the gradual and continuing addition of some substance.

70. Impastation
When the matter undergoing putrefaction thickens or congeals into the consistency of molten black pitch.

71. Impregnation
The alchemical process is sometimes paralleled with the gestation of a child. Thus impregnation follows from the union or copulation of the male and female, and leads to the generation of a new substance.

72. Inceration
The making of a substance into a soft waxy consistency, usually by combining it with water.

73. Incineration
The conversion of a substance to ashes by means of a powerful fire.

74. Incorporation
The mingling of mixed bodies into a conglomerate mass.

75. Ingression
This occurs when substances combine in such a manner that they cannot afterwards be separated.

76. Inhumation
To bury under the earth, sometimes used to mean any process that buries the active substance in a dark earthy material. Also applied to placing a flask in the warm heat of a dung bath.

77. Liquefaction
The turning of a solid material into a liquid, either by melting or dissolving.

78. Lixiviation

The oxidation of sulphide ores by exposing them to air and water. This forms vitriols.

79. Luting

The sealing of a flask or other apparatus through the use of a lute, or resinous paste which once applied sets hard and produces an airtight seal.

80. Maturation

A general term applied to identify the appearance of a degree of perfection in the work.

81. Melting

The reduction of a metal or substance to a liquid through heating.

82. Mortification

Here the substance undergoes a kind of death, usually through a putrefaction, and seems to have been destroyed and its active power lost, but eventually is revived.

83. Multiplication

The operation by which the powder of projection has its power multiplied.

84. Precipitation

The descent of a substance out of a solution. The precipitate descends to the bottom of the flask.

85. Preparation

The process by which superfluous substances are removed from the matter and that which is wanting is added to it.

86. Projection

The throwing of a ferment or tincture onto a substance in order to effect a transformation of the substance.

87. Prolectation
The separation of a substance into a subtle and more coarse part by the thinning or rarefaction of the subtler parts of the substance, rather than the coarsening of the earthy part.

88. Pulverisation
The breaking down of a substance to smaller fragments through being repeatedly struck with a blunt instrument, such as a hammer, or mallet.

89. Purgation
The purging or purifying of a sustance by it casting forth a gross part.

90. Putrefaction
The rotting of a substance, often under a prolonged gentle moist heat. Usually the matter becomes black.

91. Quinta Essentia
The making of a quintessence, or highly elevated form of a substance.

92. Rarefaction
The making of a substance extremely subtle or thin and airy.

93. Rectification
The purification of the matter by means of repeated distillations, the distillate being again distilled.

94. Reiteration
The repetition of a process, particularly applied to circular distillation, in which the distillate is returned to the vessel, and the process continued for many cycles.

95. Resolution
This occurs when substances which are mixed together become violently separated by being placed into a solution. Thus milk is in this sense resolved by vinegar. This process is similar to coagulation.

96. Restinction

Here a substance at white heat is brought to perfection by being quenched in an exalting liquid.

97. Reverberation

An ignition or calcination at a high temperature, in a reverberating furnace.

98. Revivification

The bringing of a mortified matter back to life, or reactivating it.

99. Rubification

The making of the matter in the alchemical process from white to red.

100. Segregation

The separation of a composite substance into its parts.

101. Separation

The making of two opposite components separate from each other. Often alternated with the conjunction process.

102. Stratification

An operation which produces layers in the substance in the flask.

103. Subduction

The separation of abstraction downward of the subtle part, as in filtration.

104. Sublimation

This occurs when a solid is heated and gives off a vapour which condenses on the cool upper parts of the vessel as a solid, not going through a liquid phase. An example is sal ammoniac.

105. Subtilation

The separation of the subtle part of a substance from the gross.

106. Transudation
This occurs if the essence appears to sweat out in drops during a descending distillation.

107. Trituration
The reduction of a substance to a powder, not necessarily by the use of grinding, but by the application of heat.

108. Vitrification
The making of a substance into a glass but strong heating and sometimes the addition of lime.

109. Vitriolification
The making of a vitriol. Most often from a metal by the direct action of oil of vitriol, but sometimes by a more indirect route.

THANK YOU

Thank you for taking this journey.

Whether you have carefully worked through each exercise, contemplated the philosophical foundations, or begun experimenting in your own laboratory, your willingness to engage sincerely with the Art is what truly matters.

Alchemy unfolds not merely through reading, but through practice, reflection, and lived experience. If this workbook has provided clarity, structure, or insight into your own Work, then it has fulfilled its purpose.

If you found value in this volume, I would be grateful if you would consider leaving a brief review. Your thoughts not only help other serious students find reliable instruction, but they also support the continued development of future volumes in the Peacock Publishing Workbook Series.

You may access the review page by scanning the QR code below. Your feedback is greatly appreciated!

ACKNOWLEDGMENTS

I would like to extend my sincere gratitude to those who have supported and influenced this work over the years.

To my alchemical teachers of the past three decades: thank you for your instruction, your discipline, and your encouragement. You challenged me to approach alchemy not merely as study, but as a deeply personal path of transformation.

To my students, past and present: each of you has taught me something invaluable. Through your questions, your dedication, and your growth, I have grown as well. In watching you develop your understanding of herbs, alchemy, magic, and yourselves, I have come to better understand myself. We are all the better for the Work we have shared.

To Soror MIMM and Soror IA, thank you for proofreading and for patiently deciphering what occasionally resembled inspired chaos more than structured prose.

To Adam McLean, I am grateful for your permission to reproduce the Alchemical Processes list included in the Appendix of this volume.

And finally, to my children — Bria, Sena, Aidan, Lleyton, Molly, and Elizabeth — you are my greatest teachers. In the laboratory of life, you have shaped and refined me more than any text or process ever could. You are my living stones, my elixirs of joy, my magnum opus. I love you beyond measure.

ABOUT THE AUTHOR

Frater M.T.O. has been a lifelong student of the spiritual and natural mysteries, and a practicing Alchemist, Magician, and Occultist for over three decades. His work approaches alchemy as a living, operative science—one that unites laboratory practice and inner transformation through disciplined study, patience, and experience.

He has studied within several schools of alchemy and is a member of the International Alchemy Guild, having completed the Guild's Alchemy Study Program as well as the Philosophers of Nature coursework. His practice emphasizes traditional alchemical operations, spagyric medicine, and the subtle inner changes that arise naturally through sustained work with matter, symbol, and will.

Frater M.T.O. serves as Chief Adept of the Order of the Golden Dawn in the Outer, where he guides students in the foundational principles of Western esoteric practice, initiation, and inner alchemy. Through teaching, writing, and hands-on instruction, his work seeks to preserve alchemy as a disciplined path of transformation rather than a purely symbolic or philosophical abstraction.

He has taught classes on alchemy and related esoteric arts to hundreds of students and has been a featured guest on blogs, podcasts, and radio programs exploring the practical, historical, and mystical dimensions of the Art. He is the creator of Alembic Alchemy, a long-running alchemy blog with thousands of subscribers, and the founder of an online alchemy academy dedicated to serious students of the Great Work.

He lives and works with his family and partner, Soror MIMM, continuing the Great Work through study, teaching, writing, and quiet labor in the laboratory—committed to keeping alchemy a living, transformative Art.

THE ALCHEMY WORKBOOK SERIES OF BOOKS

Available and planned titles include:

Alchemical Theory: Unlocking the Mysteries of Alchemy
Herbal Alchemy: A Practical Manual of Spagyrics
Herbal Alchemy: Spagyric Medicines
Herbal Alchemy: Creating the 7 Planetary Stones
Mineral Alchemy: Making an Alchemical Stone Elixir
Mineral Alchemy: Constructing an Artificial Stone
Magical Alchemy: Working with Herbal Spirits
Magical Alchemy: Ritual Alchemy of the Golden Dawn
Masonic Alchemy: The Sprig of Acacia

An updated list of currently available as well as planned titles can be found at the website: peacockpublishing.net.

FINIS!

SOLVE ET COAGULA!

www.ingramcontent.com/pod-product-compliance
Lightning Source LLC
Chambersburg PA
CBHW071352090426

42738CB00012B/3087